YADA YAHOWAH

WRITTEN IN STONE

CRAIG WINN

Ver. 20241121

About the Author…

Twenty-three years ago, Craig Winn was an entrepreneur. The turbulent story of his last adventure is shared in his first book, *In The Company*. It is an entertaining read, providing an eyewitness account into the culture of a private and then public company.

After the Islamic suicide bombings of 9.11.01, Craig met with al Qaeda and wrote *Tea with Terrorists* to explain – *Who they are, Why they kill, and What will stop them*. His most widely read book, *Prophet of Doom – Islam's Terrorist Dogma in Muhammad's Own Words* has now been updated and substantially expanded, becoming *God Damn Religion* after witnessing the sadistic savagery of Muslims on 10.07.23 in Israel. The resulting assessment of Islam is irrefutable because the deplorable nature of this death cult was revealed by reordering the *Quran* chronologically and setting it into the context of Muhammad's life using the earliest and most credible *Hadith*, notably Al-Tabari's *Tarikh* | History and Ibn Ishaq's *Sirat Rasul Allah* | Life of Allah's Messenger. Also, by citing the Torah and Prophets, he has conclusively demonstrated that Allah was invented in the 6th century CE and is not God, much less, Yahowah, the God of Abraham and Moses. If you want to know why fundamentalist Muslims commit 90% of the world's most heinous terrorist acts, these 5 volumes will answer your questions.

In his quest to resolve a puzzling prophetic anomaly, Craig began translating the text of the Dead Sea Scrolls. That endeavor led to the 3 volume series providing *An Introduction to God*, the 8 volumes of *Yada Yahowah*, the 5 books encouraging *Observations,* 3 exploring *Babel*, 5 for *Questioning Paul*, now *Twistianity*, and then to the 3 volumes devoted to *Coming Home*. Throughout, Mr. Winn has been committed to providing amplified translations, which are not only more accurate and complete, they are readily verified. As a result, he has been afforded thousands of unique insights into the words Yahowah inspired, many of which are unheralded and profound.

Beyond his books, Craig Winn has been interviewed as an expert on religion, politics, and current events on over 5,000 talk radio programs and has hosted 5,000 more, leaving a vast quantity of archived shows from Shattering Myths to Yada Yah Radio. He currently produces a live podcast every Friday evening, where he discusses insights gleaned from his translations.

Mr. Winn is not a theologian, nor is he associated with any religious or political institution. He does not accept donations or receive financial backing from anyone. Everything he has written is shared freely online. Even his 35 printed books are offered without royalty.

Craig has devoted his life to exploring Yahowah's revelations. He enjoys God's company and is enriched by the experience. If you have an open mind and a desire to learn, you will enjoy his translations and insights.

He encourages readers to share his translations and resulting conclusions, albeit with two important caveats: 1) You may not use them to promote any religious, political, or conspiratorial agenda. And 2) You may not use them to incite or engage in a violent act. When it comes to exposing errant and counterproductive ideas, wield words wisely.

You may contact Craig at YadaYah.com. He enjoys constructive criticism and will engage with readers. But be forewarned: he is immune to religious idiocy and will not respond to threats or taunts. The YadaYah.com site provides links to his books, to Yada Yah Radio, to many of his audio archives, as well as to friends and forums.

Lastly, Craig has a bias and an agenda. He knows and respects Yahowah, and he has devoted his life to advancing God's primary objective: which is to call His people home.

WRITTEN IN STONE

Table of Contents:

1

Yatsa' | Delivered

I Am Yahowah…

In our quest to get to *"yada'* – know" Yahowah and to *"byn* – understand" what He is offering and expecting in return, this is an ideal time to consider the Three Statements and Seven Instructions Yahowah chiseled in stone. On the First of Two Tablets, God summarized His message to humankind, providing an essential perspective from which to observe His Towrah.

On the Second Tablet, our Father explained how to live a fulfilling and rewarding life, providing instructions whose implications are more spiritual than material. Within these statements, Yahowah affirmed the terms and conditions of His Covenant – the Family-Oriented Relationship Agreement which is central to His purpose in creating us.

There are no "commandments" listed on either Tablet. Only one of the Seven Instructions and none of the Three Statements were written in the imperative mood, which typically conveys volition but can, on rare occasions, denote a command. This lone exception, which addresses our relationship with our Mother and Father, is the most familial in nature, further underscoring the absurdity of labeling these statements "commandments."

In this light, just as there is a distinction between guidance and demands, there is a difference between morality and legality. Morality regulates good and bad behavior. It resides in our *neshamah* | conscience and provides internal guidance on the inception and continuance of behavior, which can be good or bad, altruistic or selfish, beneficial or counterproductive. Moral choices play out under the auspices of freewill, prompting us to either expand upon or constrain our actions based on how we process the resulting satisfaction or guilt in context with our prior conditioning. Our decisions are predicated upon the guidance we have been given, whether from God or man, and the responses we are experiencing. Morality, therefore, can be taught but not commanded. Such is the case with the Instructions Yahowah inscribed on these Tablets.

Legality is the opposite because it is externally imposed. It is regulated by a detailed code of conduct replete with established consequences for those who are caught violating the judicial standard of those wielding political, religious, or military power. Laws are obligatory, and they are levied without the consent of those they seek to control. Punishments for violating them, regardless of one's motivations or choices, ignorance or knowledge, are levied without the consent of the perpetrator – thus negating freewill. Under such systems, behaviors are initiated and perpetuated based on an assessment of the potential gain, the likelihood of getting caught, in addition to the severity of the penalty that will be imposed by those in positions of authority.

In order to view Yahowah's Instructions from the proper perspective, it is important that we appreciate the difference between moral guidance and legal constructs, especially since one is nurtured and the other dictated. Legality demands obedience while morality is volitional. Legality is restricted to limiting bad behavior while morality serves to encourage beneficial responses. Legality is common among nations while morality varies among individuals. Legality is the product of laws while morality is the result of choices. Morality is determined by our conscience and contemplation, while legality is directed by the edicts of the empowered and reflects their ambitions.

Beyond the moral implications or legal ramifications, loving relationships like the one depicted on the Two Tablets, are consensual and can neither be imposed nor legislated. Mutually beneficial relationships thrive when informed, rational, and moral individuals are free to express themselves and contribute. They become disingenuous if either party is ordered to obey. As such, ultimatums destroy moral relationships and yet underlie all judicial systems.

From a broader perspective, the gift of freewill precludes Yahowah from commanding us to do anything. Then by offering us a *neshamah* | conscience, guidance became necessary. Therefore, these Ten Statements were offered such that we might use evidence and reason to reflect on Yahowah's purpose while benefiting from His intent.

It is also interesting that, with few exceptions, these Instructions were written using the imperfect conjugation. This has a profound influence because the imperfect is deployed to address consistent, continual, and habitual actions, which are ongoing and play out over time. As a result, we are being asked to avoid continually killing or habitually deceiving – rather than being told that we can never do either under any circumstance. Continually coveting and then routinely stealing that which does not belong to us (as is the case with national entitlements) and consistently bearing false witness (which is the result of political correctness and conspiracy), is a recipe for an unfulfilling and counterproductive life.

Before we press on, there is yet another insight I'd like to share which may help us appreciate the nature of these Three Statements and Seven Instructions. While loving relationships are initiated and perpetuated under the auspices of freewill, they thrive and grow with structure. They become synergistic, with their overall value becoming greater than the sum of individuals, when each can be relied upon to contribute and share in a manner which is dependable and mutually beneficial. It is both our common values and different interests which make relationships interesting.

Therefore, the Towrah establishes the framework for abundantly fulfilling and intellectually satisfying lives. God's guidance seeks to capitalize upon our unique proclivities and insights while encouraging us to experience the attitudes and aptitudes of others. These Statements and Instructions were designed to harmoniously bring uncommon people together with a shared moral compass while enriching everyone's experience. The message of the Two Tablets is that, while we are not the same, we can become perfect together so long as we embrace these principles, making our differences a cause of celebration rather than conflict.

It is my hope, and I expect Yah's as well, that once we have concluded our review of His Three Statements and Seven Instructions, we will better appreciate what God is offering and expecting in return. We will be properly equipped to engage in the relationship He envisioned within the structure He conceived such that we will be able to celebrate the resulting synergism.

As we press forward, these translations will continue to be amplified, providing us with a richer rendition of Yahowah's advice. In addition, they will include the Hebrew words upon which these renderings are based because it remains important that we take the time to verify their authenticity.

Turning to Yahowah's testimony, we find...

"Then (*wa*), **God** (*'elohym* – the Almighty; plural of *'elowah*) **conveyed** (*dabar* – communicated, spoke, and wrote, provided instruction and direction with (piel imperfect consecutive – the subject, God, causes the object, these words, to be effective, enabling and empowering them with ongoing and unfolding implications over time as a function of His will)) **all of** (*kol* – every one of) **these statements using words** (*ha dabarym* – these accounts, this message and declaration)**, in our presence** (*'eth* – in association with us and in proximity to us)**, providing perspective** (*ha 'eleh* – from a relatively close vantage point, conveying God's view)**, by saying** (*'amar* – explaining, claiming, answering, counseling, warning, and promising)**:...**" (*Shemowth* / Names / Exodus 20:1)

Let's begin by considering the nature of a word that has become unnecessarily controversial, *'elohym* – which is the plural of the prolonged emphatic, *'elowah*. It is a noun, serving as a title, but it is not a name. Keeping in mind that Hebrew does not have lower and uppercase variations of its alphabet, its English equivalents are "god," "gods" or "God" depending on who it is addressing.

Religious Jews have been beguiled into writing "G-d" because Yahowah said not to memorialize the names of false "*'elohym* – gods." However, God is not Yahowah's name, and it is not the name of a false god, either. Moreover, we know that Yahowah is not concerned about us saying the names of false gods because He has set an undeniable and irrefutable example of referring to *Ba'al* | the Lord and *'Asherah* | the Blessed, albeit always to expose and condemn them.

While there has never been a god named God, one was named "Gad." Further, Gad serves as the name of one of the twelve tribes of Yisra'el. And since it cannot be spoken or written without conveying the name of the false Gad, the religious argument is moot. Additionally, the Canaanites named their supreme deity, "*'El*," turning this title into an improper designation – thereby making *'el* a dirty word if we were to follow the rabbinical reasoning.

5

Driving to the heart of its intended meaning, a similar word such as *'aluw*, which shares its first three letters in common with *'elowah* (recognizing that the concluding *ah* simply makes the title feminine), means "to behold, to look up and to pay attention" – the best perspective when it comes to knowing Yah. It is also interesting that *'el* is a preposition, meaning "to and toward, regarding and concerning, on account of and according to" and thereby properly directs our attention toward Yah. As a noun, *'el* speaks of "power, strength, and might," and thus of "capability and influence." It is from *'el* that translators extrapolate "Mighty One" or "Almighty." And yet, this may not be the most accurate rendering because *'el* is derived from *'ayl* (often transliterated *'ayil*) which differs only in the addition of the hand of God "⊃" in the Ancient Hebrew script.

'Ayl is particularly descriptive, conveying a great deal about our Creator. It denotes a "ram," and thus "male lamb," thereby depicting God as one with His flock. *'Ayl* is also an "upright pillar," which was set in the center of the Tent of the Witness and used to enlarge and secure the Tabernacle.

Along these same lines, *'ayl* / *'ayil* is used to describe the "doorpost used to secure and hinge the opening," once again taking us to the Doorway of the Tabernacle and Life itself. Entry through these doors is made possible by the sacrifice of the *Pesach 'ayl*. Lastly, an *'ayil* is a "strong man who leads his people as if a king." This points us to Dowd, Yah's beloved son, His anointed Messiah and King, and most notably in this case, both God's chosen *Ra'ah* | Shepherd and *Zarowa'* | Sacrificial Lamb. As such, an *'ayl* is someone with the "strength, might, power, and will to provide assistance, to help others in a meaningful and productive manner."

The letters which comprise *'elowah* are equally revealing: 𐤀𐤅𐤋𐤄. The Aleph - 𐤀 was drawn in the shape of a ram's head, verifying the connections we have made by examining the root, ꓕꙨ - 'ayl. God is striving to be one with His flock.

The Lamed - ꓘ is a shepherd's staff, and reveals that Yahowah wants to guide, nurture, and protect His sheep, to walk and explore along with His flock, camping out together.

The third letter in 'elowah, the Wah - Y, is a tent peg. It represents the implement used to increase the size and security of the Tabernacle, which is symbolic of Yah's home. In addition, the Wah is used to make connections between thoughts such that the benefits increase synergistically.

The concluding letter in Yahowah's preferred title, Hey - ꙮ, shows an observant and engaged individual standing up, reaching up, and looking up to God. This also makes "'elowah – God" a feminine title, not unlike His Towrah, His Ruwach, and His name, Yahowah.

Considering all of these things, from being a lamb among His flock, a caring and protective shepherd, the source of empowering connections for those who engage and are observant, it seems a bit trite to simply write "God.' And yet, aren't these the attributes we should want our God to project?

Religious institutions are wont to call what follows "The Ten Commandments." But according to their Author, He "dabar – conveyed and communicated" "dabarym – statements using words." These "declarations" are not numbered, and He never refers to them as "commandments" for the reasons we have and will continue to discuss.

Few things are as relevant to developing a relationship with God as knowing what these statements and instructions actually convey and then coming to appreciate how they apply to the conditions of the Covenant. The proper approach to living a productive and satisfying life, one that leads to heaven, is presented on these Tablets.

Digging deeper, "*dabar* – conveyed" was scribed using the piel stem which tells us that God's "*dabarym* – words" are actionable. They instruct and direct, guide and teach, influencing the observant. In the imperfect, we discover that God is continuing to speak to us through His Word. And in the consecutive, these Statements and Instructions convey Yahowah's will.

With this introduction noted, and realizing that Hebrew is written right to left, on the top right of the First of these Two Stone Tablets, the Creator of the universe and Author of life, introduced Himself and then inscribed...

"**'I am** (*'anky*) **Yahowah** (*Yahowah* – from the Hebrew vowels Y-aH-oW-aH, or 𐤅𐤄𐤅𐤉 in the earliest Ancient Hebrew script)**, your God** (*'elohym 'atah* – your shepherd, a ram among the sheep, and the doorway to an expansive and abundant life for those who are engaged, standing up, reaching up, and looking up (suffixed in the second-person singular)) **who, for the benefit of the relationship** (*'asher* – who to show the correct and narrow path to get the most out of life) **brought you out and delivered you** (*yatsa' 'atah* – descended to serve you, extending Myself to guide you, doing everything which is required to lead those who respond to Me, including disseminating the information needed broadly, openly, and publicly such that they can be led (hifil perfect – at a moment in time God engaged with us in such a way that we were empowered to come out)) **away from the realm** (*min 'erets* – out of the land, region, territory, nation, and country) **of the Crucibles of Religious and Political Oppression** (*Mitsraym* – of the cauldrons of governmental, military, economic, and conspiratorial coercion and cruelty, where the people were confined, restricted, and persecuted; plural of *matsowr* – to be treated as a foe and

8

besieged during a time of testing and tribulation; from *tsuwr* – to be bound and constrained by an adversary, besieged and assaulted, as if in a concentration camp by those showing great hostility)**, out of the house** (*min beyth* – from the home, household, family, and place) **of slavery** (*'ebed* – of worship and servitude, of bondage and working for one's salvation, of government authority and religious officials)**.** (20:2)

You shall not continue to exist with (*lo' hayah la 'atah* – you shall not always be, neither function nor move toward, arise, live, nor appear with (qal imperfect – continually and literally)) **other** (*'acher* – someone else's, different, extra, another, or additional) **gods** (*'elohym*) **over and above** (*'al* – elevated beyond, in proximity to or near, before, or in addition to) **My presence** (*paneh 'any* – My appearance or face)**.'"** (*Shemowth* / Names / Exodus 20:2-3)

Yahowah began by spelling out His name so that we might know it, etching "𐤉𐤄𐤅𐤄" (pronounced Y-aH-oW-aH) in stone. It would, therefore, be irrational to believe that He does not care what we call Him or that He wanted His name removed from His Tablets and replaced with "the LORD." It would be ignorant to believe that every word which follows "Yahowah" on these Tablets could be read before the people, but that Moseh could not pronounce the name of God as scholars insist.

It would be rational to conclude that, since Yahowah wrote His name before providing any instruction, His identity is paramount to knowing Him and benefiting from what He is offering. And that is a devastating realization for religious Jews and Christians because each has discounted Yahowah's name from the beginning.

Let's take the opportunity to reinforce something we have already noted. The first words Yahowah etched in stone conclusively demonstrate that "Yahowah" is God's

9

name and that "God" is His title. While He has a number of titles and a marvelous array of attributes, God has only one name: the one He chiseled in stone. He will not respond to any other designation, including "Jesus" or "Christ," "HaShem" or "'Adonai," the "Lord" or "Allah."

For all of the Christians and Jews who have paid homage to the "Ten Commandments," believing that they were honoring God by erecting monuments to them, by citing grossly incomplete and inaccurate variations of what Yahowah said, by removing His name and replacing it with "I am the Lord," I can assure you that He is not amused. His name was the second thing He wrote, placing it between "I am" and "your God," so it was hard to miss. Just think of the hubris and audacity of men and women believing that it is appropriate to not only edit what Yahowah wrote, changing it to their liking, but to replace His name with one He commonly uses to identify the Adversary.

Following His introduction, Yahowah, our God, deployed *'asher* to make an important point regarding "the beneficial relationship" He intended and the "correct way to get the most out of life." While it is dismissed by religious translators with a simplistic "who," *'asher* is among the most edifying words in the whole of the Hebrew lexicon.

Appearing as the fourth term Yahowah wrote on our behalf, *'asher* can be a relative particle, a conjunction, a pronoun, a preposition, a noun, and a name. In addition, *'asher* is also a verb. It can be rendered as "which, what, who, when, or where," such that it serves to "establish a relationship between things," including between our God and ourselves. As a masculine noun, it depicts "a blessing and good fortune, a joyous and happy attitude." As a feminine noun, *'asher* speaks of "walking along the correct and restrictive path to give meaning to life." It describes "the proper place to stand to be stable and secure." As a

10

name, 'Asher was one of Ya'aqob's sons and thus part of Yisra'el.

The actionable, or verbal, form of *'asher* is the most revealing. To *'asher* is "to live an upright life, to walk in a straightforward manner, to be led and then to guide." To *'asher* is "to speak well of someone, commending them, to pronounce them blessed, happy, and prosperous." To *'asher* is "to encourage correct thinking and good behavior through accurate teaching."

In the language of relationships, *'asher* makes many of the most important connections – just as it is doing on this occasion. Here it was written to convey that Yahowah has done all that is required to free us from the crucibles of human oppression. All we need to do is recognize who He is and what He expects and then walk away from them with Him. It is the proper path to get the most out of life.

Those who wish to live commendable, prosperous, and happy lives should follow His lead out of *Mitsraym* | the Crucibles of Religious and Political Oppression, of Military and Economic Persecution. Yahowah is presenting Himself as our liberator and savior – the one who is offering to free us from all forms of servitude. The fact is men subjugate and oppress by imposing dictates people must obey. God offers to free us from them.

Since it is something that is often missed, let's be clear: Yahowah *yatsa'* | withdrew the Children of Yisra'el from "*mitsraym* – the political despots and religious tyrants within the cauldrons of military and economic subjugation," away from "the authority figures in the place of coercive cruelty where, as slaves, they were confined and restricted by societal subjugation and subject to a caste system."

Mitsraym is the plural of *matsowr*, which is "to be delineated as a foe and besieged during a time of testing and tribulation." It in turn is derived from "*tsuwr* – to be bound and confined by an adversary, to be assaulted, shut up, and enclosed as if in a concentration camp by those showing great hostility."

By telling the Children of Yisra'el that He was *yatsa'* | leading them away from *mitsraym* | political, societal, cultural, conspiratorial, and religious oppression, which is based upon "*tsuwr* – being besieged and assaulted in troubling fashion," Yahowah was actually predicting another *Yatsa'* | Exodus – the second one from the time of *Ya'aqob's Tsuwr* | Israel's Troubles. This period of unprecedented abuse of Jews worldwide will commence in the years preceding Yahowah's return for His people on *Yowm Kipurym* | the Day of Reconciliations in year 6000 Yah, at sunset in Yaruwshalaim, Yisra'el, October 2nd, 2033.

While it was important to remind Yisra'el that He had saved them by removing them from the worst of human oppression, it is also likely that Yahowah was trying to forewarn His people, such that they were ready and waiting for His return. Additionally, by inscribing this as the initial statement on the First Tablet, Yahowah is unequivocally stating that man oppresses and that He liberates. Religion is humankind's most restrictive and abusive foe while Yahowah, His Towrah and Covenant are the only effective remedies.

It would be impossible to overstate the importance of accepting this perspective on the difference between God and man. They have the opposite intent and their influence, the opposite effect.

Further, Yahowah wrote this for His people, not for Haredim, Christians, Muslims, Hindus, Buddhists, or Socialist Secular Humanists. You cannot be one of His people by opposing them.

The first verb, "*yatsa'* – I brought you out," was scribed using the hifil stem while bearing the perfect conjugation. Collectively, they enable us to better understand how we are expected to respond to the benefits Yahowah is presenting. With the hifil stem, the object of the verb in this case, those God is leading away from man's influence, participates in the action, which is being saved by Him. Therefore, to benefit from God's willingness to deliver us from national influences, we must accept Yahowah's guidance. Such is the nature of the Covenant Relationship, where we must engage to participate.

By using the perfect conjugation, Yahowah is revealing that He has done everything, leaving nothing to be done except for us to engage. The perfect denotes a completed action irrespective of time. It reveals that God would, and now has, and eventually will "descend to serve us, extending Himself to guide us, so that those who respond will be led away from the crucibles of human coercion." Therefore, when we reflect upon the full implications of the way *yatsa'* was written, God said: "I have done everything to lead those who respond away from" the ill effects of government and religious subjugation.

His words provide critical information we must act upon to exist in His presence. We need to know that there is a God, that His name is Yahowah, and that He authored His Towrah for us. He "*yatsa'* – descended to serve us, extending Himself to guide us, doing what was needed to lead us away" from human oppression, including "broadly, openly, and publicly disseminating the information needed for us to be free." This means that He positioned Himself serving us, working as our savior and guide, personally leading us away from works-based salvation schemes. It is a perspective that is monumentally important because it is the opposite of what religions would have us believe. This means that those who are bowing down to God, who are lifting Him up in praise, and who believe they are serving Him, have got it all wrong. Yahowah is both willing and able to help us and wants His children to capitalize on what He has done.

Should you not see the symbolism of "*mitsraym* – crucibles" representing governmental, cultural, religious, economic, conspiratorial, and military oppression, God spells it out for us with "*beyth 'ebed* – the house of slavery and bondage." These are the only means of institutionalized subjugation and the suppression of freewill. Enslavement is simply the lowest rung on the caste systems which have been pervasive throughout man's history.

The second verb, "*hayah* – to exist," was modified with *lo'*, serving as a form of negation, thereby, nullifying a person's existence who is unwilling to let go of the platitudes which bind the masses to human institutions. It was suffixed with *la*, a preposition meaning "to, toward, or concerning," telling us that there is a consequence if we move in one direction or another. In addition, *hayah* was suffixed in the third-person singular: "you," revealing that these words affect us.

More than this, *hayah* was written using the qal stem and imperfect conjugation. This stem speaks of that which is genuine and should be interpreted literally. Meanings are matter-of-fact rather than nuanced. This distinguishes the qal stem from something which is hypothetical or merely symbolic. It reads: "you literally will not exist." As the voice of relationships, the qal stem reveals that we, as the subject of the verb, are affected by its action which is the termination of our continued existence. That is to say that our soul's survival is predicated upon our response to this statement.

Further, rather than using the perfect conjugation as God did with *yatsa'*, *hayah* was scribed in the imperfect. It means that there is an ongoing consequence of this statement which will endure. And while that suggests we

14

should be careful in our considerations, the good news is that since *hayah* was written in the imperfect, the moment we walk away from our devotion to religion or politics, and our affinity toward societal customs or the military, we are no longer at odds with this statement.

Hayah is as important as any word in the whole of God's Word. It serves as the basis of Yahowah's name – explaining what 𐤉𐤄𐤅𐤄 means. In Ancient Hebrew, *hayah* was written 𐤄𐤉𐤄. It reveals that we should be standing up, not on our knees, looking up rather than heads bowed, reaching up to God rather than hands clasped in prayer. Then when Yah offers His outstretched hand, we are ready to grasp hold so that He can lift us up and take us home.

Furthermore, *hayah* speaks of time, which is especially relevant in Hebrew where every verb is liberated in the fourth dimension – as time exists in the past, present, and future simultaneously. In this light, please note that this verb is a palindrome, reading the same way right to left as it does left to right, thereby expressing endless possibilities. No longer stuck in the ordinary flow of time, *hayah*, just like Yahowah, promises a different form of liberation, one in which we live forever and travel wherever and whenever we desire. Those who choose to accept the God who scribed these words will no longer be as we currently are, slowly moving away from the past into the future while stuck on this rock we call Earth. Liberated, indeed.

Since the verb, *hayah*, means "to exist," and speaks of "being" irrespective of time, by negating it as *lo'* does in this case, the statement reveals that those who embrace other gods will "cease to exist." And that is because false gods will never be tolerated in Yah's presence. That is what *She'owl* is for, not *Shamaym*.

It is also telling that *lo' hayah-la 'aher 'elohym 'al-paneh 'any* is a simple statement of fact. It is not a command much less a commandment. Rather than commanding: "You must not go to Venus," it is similar to saying: "You cannot breathe the air on Venus." God is stating that since false notions cease to exist in His presence, the same fate applies to those who believe in them.

At this point, Yahowah has not asked much of those who wish to live in His presence. We must simply refer to Him by name, follow His lead away from institutionalized oppression, and recognize that He, alone, is God.

However, recognizing the extent men have gone to over the ages to corrupt His message, considering the sorry state of Bible translations, what chance does anyone have of coming to know Yahowah as He revealed Himself? When those who have claimed to have been trustworthy have been so disingenuous, the truth is hard to find. And sadly, erroneous data leads to invalid conclusions.

The First Statement on the First Tablet reads:

"Then, Almighty God conveyed, communicating by enabling and empowering all of these statements comprised of words in our presence, providing perspective, saying and explaining: (*Shemowth* 20:1)

'I am Yahowah, your God (a ram among the sheep and your shepherd, your doorway to an expansive and abundant life) who, to show the correct path to get the most out of life, brought you out and delivered you, descending to serve you by doing everything which was required to lead those who respond away from the crucibles of political, religious, economic, and military oppression, out of the house of slavery, the place of worship and servitude, of bondage and working for one's salvation, and of man's authority. (*Shemowth* 20:2)

16

You shall not continue to exist with other, different or additional, gods over and above My presence.'" (*Shemowth* / Names / Exodus 20:3)

Men who falsely claimed that they were authorized by God, published: "And God spake all these words, saying, (20:1) I am the LORD thy God, which have brought thee out of the land of Egypt, out of the house of bondage. (20:2) Thou shalt have no other gods before me." (Exodus 20:3 KJV)

Is there an Individual or Statement more inappropriate to edit or truncate? Is there a decision more vital than the eternal fate of our soul? So how do you suppose Yahowah is going to respond when it comes to holding the religious editors and publishers, scholars and theologians, pastors and priests, accountable for what they have done to make it difficult, if not nearly impossible, to correctly respond to the Creator?

In a world which has distanced itself from overt expressions of paganism, while still wallowing in its myths and symbols, this statement may not resonate sufficiently to save the religious. After mislabeling these statements as "Commandments," religious institutions have universally skipped over Yahowah's name, the relationship He established with us, and the role He personally plays in our salvation only to misrepresent *hayah* to say, "you shall not have" as opposed to "you shall not exist." Those are a lot of mistakes considering that we've only considered the first twenty Hebrew words Yahowah inscribed on these tablets.

𐤋𐤅𐤄𐤉

The Second of the Three Statements Yahowah etched in stone on the First of the Two Tablets conveys a wide range of things relatively few people have considered. As you contemplate the implications of God's comprehensive presentation in this regard, compare them to man's abridged "You shall not make a graven image" to appreciate just how egregiously the unwary have been cheated.

"**'You should not continue to associate yourself with or engage on behalf of** (*lo' 'asah la 'atah* – you should not make a practice of attending to or doing anything with, you should not act upon or involve yourself with, you should not fashion or profit from, you should not conceive, acquire, celebrate, or work around (qal imperfect – conveying a literal interpretation and ongoing implications of acting and engaging on behalf of)) **a religious image or object of worship** (*pesel* – a shaped, sculpted, carved, cast, chiseled, or designed icon and idol associated with the divine, a representation of any god)**, or any** (*wa kol* – or any kind or variation of a) **visual representation of something** (*tamunah* – likeness, appearance, picture, drawing, painting, or form which depicts or resembles, attempting to establish any relationship by way of a substitution (such as the Christian depiction of a Dead God on a Stick or Judaism's Star of David)) **which is in the heavens above** (*'asher ba ha shamaym min ma'al* – that is within the spiritual realm on high or displayed throughout the universe including the sun, moon, planets, and stars above (thereby eliminating all sun, lunar, and astrology imagery and flags with stars)) **which is on the earth below** (*wa 'asher ba ha 'erets min tahath* – which is associated with the land and ground, even the material realm (thus destroying the deification of men or devotion to environmentalism))**, or which is in the waters** (*wa 'asher ba ha maym*) **beneath the land** (*min tahath la ha 'erets* – from below the ground). (*Shemowth* 20:4)

You should not speak about them on your own initiative nor make a practice of bowing down and

worshiping them (*lo' chawah la hem* – you should not continue to promote their message on your own accord or display their words because such uncoerced and ongoing verbal declarations and announcements will influence you, you should not religiously prostrate yourself in obeisance and homage to them, show any allegiance to them on an ongoing basis, nor habitually worship them, especially if not compelled or forced (hitpael imperfect jussive – acting without any compulsion, habitually or continually responding to the will of the religious influences)), **and you shall not habitually serve them or compel anyone to be passionate about them** (*wa lo' 'abad hem* – you should not continually work or labor in their cause or make a career of working as their ministers, you should not submit to them in servitude nor encourage anyone else to do so, neither should you act upon them nor consistently engage with them (hofal imperfect – you should not make a habit of forcing, encouraging, nor compelling anyone to act or serve on their behalf)).

For, indeed (*ky* – because and emphasizing this point), **I** (*'anky*), **Yahowah** (*Yahowah* – the proper pronunciation of YaHoWaH, our *'elowah* – God as directed in His *ToWRaH* – teaching regarding His *HaYaH* – existence and our *ShaLoWM* – restoration), **your God** (*'elohy 'atah*), **am a fiercely protective, steadfastly loyal, and jealous God** (*qana' 'el* – a God who is desirous of exclusivity in a devoted relationship, a God who is passionate and extremely defensive of those He zealously loves, going above and beyond to acquire His creation so as to bring forth new life), **actually counting and reckoning** (*paqad* – literally taking stock of and genuinely recording, assigning, depositing, and considering (qal participle – a highly descriptive inventory with literal implications)) **the perversity of twisting and distorting** (*'awon* – the depravity of perverting and manipulating, deviating from the way, the guilt and punishment derived from delusions and depravity, the liability for unfaithfulness and wrongdoing) **of the fathers** (*'aby*) **upon the children** (*'al ben* – over the sons) **concerning** (*'al*) **the third and the fourth generations** (*silesym wa 'al ribea'*) **of those who shun Me because they dislike Me** (*sane' 'any* – of those who are openly hostile and adverse toward Me, who abhor, hate, detest, and loathe Me, literally striving maliciously against Me, snubbing Me by refusing to engage in a relationship with Me (qal participle – serving as a literal and vivid depiction of an abhorrent behavior)). (*Shemowth* 20:5)

However (*wa*), **I will genuinely act and actually engage to literally prepare, perform, and produce** (*'asah* – I will actively effect and appoint, offer and celebrate, and I will demonstrate by doing what is required to deliver on behalf of those who respond (qal participle – literally and demonstrably engaging through)) **loyal and devoted love, unfailing mercy, unearned favor, and genuine kindness** (*chesed* – actual forgiveness, steadfast and ardent appreciation, a friendly and affectionate relationship, faithfulness and goodness) **on behalf of** (*la'* – to enable the approach of) **thousands** (*'elephym*) **who move toward Me and love Me** (*la 'ahab 'any* – who form a close and affectionate, loving and friendly, familial relationship with Me, coming to know and like Me, who come to prefer Me and find an association with Me desirable) **and also** (*wa* – in addition) **who approach Me by closely observing and carefully considering** (*la shamar* – who enter My presence by becoming observant and actually focusing upon, thoroughly examining, and thoughtfully evaluating (qal participle)) **My instructions and directions, terms and conditions** (*mitswah 'any* – the verbal and written stipulations, statements, and structure which uphold My Covenant, My authoritative guidelines and codicils which serve as prescriptions for My relationship agreement and mutually binding contract; a compound of *my* – to ponder the who, what, why, when, where, and how questions regarding the *tsawah* –

20

authorized and authoritative communications, appointed and ordained mission, instructions and directions)."'" (*Shemowth* / Names / Exodus 20:4-6)

Yahowah has asked us not to be religious. God is opposed to religious imagery, opposed to religious behavior, and is antagonistic toward religious services. He is intolerant of the promotion of any message associated with any god by any other name (and that would include Allah, Jehovah, the Lord, Adonai, HaShem, the Eternal One, and Jesus Christ). The reason is straightforward and simple: Yahowah is committed to developing a loving and monogamous relationship with us. It is the very essence of His nature – something He is passionate about which is why He is personally engaged in our salvation.

As a result, Yahowah warns us about the consequence of distorting, twisting, and perverting His message – something every religion has done. By corrupting His testimony, we condemn our own children – as they are exposed to religious deceptions by someone they are naturally prone to look up to and trust.

By contrast, God has affirmed in writing that those who "*shamar* – closely observe, carefully examine, and thoughtfully consider" His instructions will "*chesed* – receive mercy – an unearned and undeserved gift" Yahowah has personally prepared and delivered. And yet, His unearned favor and unmerited kindness will be limited to one in a million people. That is precisely what "thousands" among billions conveys. As such, all popular religions have been summarily excluded as a means to receive Yahowah's mercy.

While etching this anti-religious message and its consequence in stone ought to have been more than enough to garner our attention, it was repeated in *Shemowth* / Names / Exodus 34:7, *Dabarym* / Words / Deuteronomy 5:10, and *Yirma'yah* / Jeremiah 32:18 – as well as throughout the entirety of *Yasha'yah* / Isaiah, *Zakaryah* / Zechariah, *Mal'aky* / Malachi, and the *Mizmowr* / Psalms and *Mashal* / Proverbs of the *Mashyach* | Messiah Dowd. God wants us to know that religion is hereditary, pervasive, hateful, and deadly, and the truth, while loving and merciful, is exceedingly uncommon.

Should you want to be among the few who will benefit from Yahowah's "*chesed* – mercy," please note: when God etched this advice in stone, there was but one place where His "*mitswah* – the instructions and directions, terms and conditions pertaining to His Covenant" were written: His *Towrah* | Teaching and Guidance. As a result, Yahowah's Towrah is the lone source of Yahowah's "*chesed* – unmerited, undeserved, unearned, and unfailing favor which leads to a loving relationship" with God.

Before we press on and consider what else Yahowah etched in stone, let's take this opportunity to review each of the four clauses which comprise this overtly anti-religious statement. As we just read, God wrote: **"You should not continue to associate yourself with or make a practice of attending to, you should not act upon or engage on behalf of a religious image, an object of worship, or any representation of a god, even a picture or painting depicting that which is in the heavens above, including the sun, moon, planets, and stars, or which is on the earth below, even that which is in the waters beneath the land."** (*Shemowth* 20:4)

Since these words were written by God to teach us so that we might respond appropriately to Him, the verbs which are designed to guide our actions are especially relevant. Here *'asah*, which was negated by *lo'*, was written using the qal imperfect which is to say that "we should actually refrain from continuing to engage with or habitually act upon" God's laundry list of religious objects. The qal stem dictates a literal interpretation, telling us that God is serious about us disassociating from the kind of images which permeate our world, while the imperfect conjugation refers to any behavior that is ongoing, consistent, or habitual. *Lo' 'asah* conveys: "do not serve, profit from, or engage with" religious trappings, icons, and symbols which were crafted to inspire reverence and worship.

While *'asah* can be translated as "make, conceive, or fashion" using its secondary and tertiary connotations, there are many Hebrew words which are far better suited to describe the act of conceiving, creating, building, carving, or engraving an idol. For example, "carve" in Hebrew can be written as: *qala', chaqah, chatubah, miqla'ath,* or *charosheth.* To "engrave" is: *pituwach* or *pathach.* To "create or fashion" is *bara'.* And to "build or establish" is *banah.* Therefore, with so many words which more adeptly describe the construction of a religious icon, we ought not look to the secondary or tertiary connotations of *'asah* to fill this role. This admonition is about our actions rather than our artistry.

When negated and suffixed with *la* and then shaded by the imperfect, *lo' 'asah la* teaches us "not to habitually do anything which associates ourselves with" a "*pesel* – object of worship." We are "to avoid attending to them, acting upon them, and should refrain from consistently engaging with them." Therefore, just because you never personally carved a crucifix, you are not exonerated if you are still worshiping in a church where the Dead God on a Stick is present. You would be at cross purposes with this instruction if preaching on behalf of the cross, pledging your allegiance to a flag, or feeling patriotic while standing before a political statue in a national monument. It is the ongoing observance of these symbols which God is telling us to avoid.

A "*pesel* – object of worship and religious icon" can come in many forms, from the wine and bread of Communion and the Eucharist to the crosses or crucifixes which are on prominent display in most churches. And a "*tamunah* – visual representation and likeness" is all-encompassing. It would include the pictures and busts on sanctuary walls and the images depicted in stained-glass windows. If you look closely, especially in an orthodox church, you'll notice how many references there are to the sun, moon, and stars, with circles around the crosses, halos above the heads of their saints, and starbursts embellishing objects used in church rituals. Not only are men and animals on display, both carved and painted, but the Christian god is also depicted as a man. But that is not the end of it. The pope wears a Dagon hat, symbolic of the fish god of old, and evangelicals often adorn their cars with an ICHTHUS which is also drawn in the form of a fish from the waters beneath the land.

I would like you to consider something else, something I think is directly related to an "object of worship," and that is the Christian caricature known as "the Lord Jesus Christ." The Christian god is not only modeled after pagan deities, he is depicted in the image of man. His likeness is ubiquitous in places of worship and prostration. And he is most often adorned with a halo, symbolic of the sun.

Turning to Judaism, the religious reverence for the so-called "Star of David" is appalling. There is no star associated with the Messiah anywhere in the Towrah, Naby', wa Mizmowr. Therefore, while it cannot be the "Star of David," the most infamous false Messiah in Jewish lore is *Bar Kokhba* | Son of a Star. He was the 2nd-century warlord Rabbi Akiba elevated to the status of *ha Mashyach* to lead an insurrection against Rome. He was wrong. The Diaspora was the result. This star is the legacy of that misguided religious edict.

It was under this same symbol that Jews were subjugated and demonized throughout the Holy Roman Empire, and most notably under the terrorizing influence of the Third Reich. The six-pointed star served as a ticket to the death camps across Europe. It is unconscionable that this sign of the false witness and false messiah who caused the Diaspora, and the insignia under which Jews were inhumanely abused, has become the symbol of the nation and its religion, Judaism. Its use is among the worst things Jews have ever done to degrade themselves.

God was not done condemning religion. Still focused on all forms of religious imagery and deception, He wrote: **"You should not speak about them on your own initiative or make a practice of bowing down and worshiping them, you should not continue to promote their message on your own accord or display their words because such uncoerced and ongoing verbal declarations will influence you, nor should you habitually worship them, especially if not compelled or forced, and you should not serve them or coerce anyone to be passionate about them. Do not continually work or labor in their cause nor make a career of serving as their ministers, nor encourage anyone else to do so."** (*Shemowth* 20:5)

While the opening statement was designed to distinguish the kind of images Yahowah considers inappropriate, this time it is our response to these political and religious symbols which is being discouraged. Actions in this regard are destructive to the relationship God is seeking to achieve.

To engage in the Covenant, we have to walk away from political, religious, and societal allegiances. And yet, look how often people sing national anthems to their flag, pledging to serve what it represents. By standing at attention, removing one's hat, and placing a hand over the heart while others salute, transforms this political symbol into an object of worship. Patriots honor it by bellowing out its anthem in the presence of roaring cheers. In America, the Lincoln Memorial is a shrine, a temple to a man. And the Statue of Liberty, the national image of freedom to which countless patriots opine, is the Greek goddess Athena complete with her light and sunburst crown.

Since it is our ongoing response to these deified and politicized symbols which is at issue, we should not be surprised that there are two verbs in this brief statement – both indicative of behavior God wants to be curtailed. The first, *chawah*, is high on the list of the most inaccurately rendered Hebrew terms. It is primarily used to depict "a verbal declaration and public pronouncement promoting a message, speaking for or writing about someone or something so as to let the individual or institution know what we think about them."

Secondarily, there are certain contexts, especially when negated, when *chawah* can address religious behavior such as "bowing down in worship, thereby prostrating oneself in obeisance." In this context, and negated by *lo'*, both definitions apply. Fortunately, however, *chawah* was inscribed in the imperfect conjugation because Yahowah realized that most of us would at some point in our lives make a habit of regurgitating religious prayers and platitudes, continually offering declarations of our faith, all while bowing down to and worshiping the images mankind has crafted. The Hasidic have all but nationalized this approach.

Equally insightful, *chawah* was engraved using the hitpael stem, something so rare it is only found 170 times in the Hebrew text. Known as the causative reflexive form, it reveals that the subject, which would be you and me, is influenced by the way we act with respect to the verb. Those who bow down in the presence of religious imagery will find themselves prostrate before God in judgment. Those who worship will be associated with the object of their faith. Those who speak on behalf of the gods man has created will be seen as being allied with them.

The truth is religion and politics change people, just as the military does, in a way that displeases Yah, thereby disassociating those who fall prey to their beguiling nature. But more than this, the hitpael stem addresses behaviors which are not influenced or acted upon by outside forces. Therefore, by negating it, Yahowah is telling us that He does not want us to be manipulated or coerced into religious or political allegiances or declarations, thereby helping us avoid becoming the pawns of others. He wants us to think and act independently. The hitpael stem is wholly incompatible with religious and political influence, patriotism and political correctness, as well as slavery and servitude.

The most obvious, and indeed egregious, violation of this divine edict today is the example of Catholic and Orthodox Christians reciting the Rosary or the Lord's Prayer while bowing down before and praying to one of the millions of statues of Mary whom they believe is "the Mother of God and Queen of Heaven," although those titles are both Babylonian as is the religious festival named in her honor: Easter. Another would be queuing up to recite rote prayers at the Western Wall of the Temple Mount.

By using the imperfect with "*lo' chawah la*" to say "you should not habitually issue religious declarations or make a practice of bowing down in worship, continually demonstrating your allegiance" toward what could only be construed as "political and religious symbols," Yahowah has made it easy for us to let go and walk away. The moment we stop doing and saying the things God disdains we are no longer in conflict with the Instruction.

There is one final aspect of the way "*lo' chawah* – do not continue to make declarations" which we should consider, and that is the jussive mood. Typically, the jussive denotes third-person volition, but since Yahowah wrote these in first person to us in second person, the religious objects and environment they adorn are all that could be considered third person. And should that be the case, the jussive would suggest that we not seek to do the will of religious gods.

The next verb is "*lo' 'abad* – you should not continue to serve them." Once again, Yahowah used the imperfect conjugation which speaks of habitual, ongoing behavior with unfolding consequences. But this time, He deployed the hophal stem. It is the passive counterpart to the hifil which is to say that religious imagery and political symbols influence an individual based upon how each person acts toward them. So, while religious and patriotic people actively participate in their culture's mythology, they were typically beguiled into doing so.

Religion feeds religion. The religious congregate together. They reinforce one another. They feed each other's faith. They believe the same things, say the same things, and do the same things, all while avoiding contact with those who would question them.

'Abad, as the Hebrew word for "work," depicts "the expenditure of considerable energy or intensity" toward a goal which, in this case, is being religious or political. *'Abad* also speaks of service, which today we typically associate with a religious service, public and thus political service, and military service. And while I would argue that none of these equate to providing a service because the participants are paid and the work is counterproductive, I'd like to draw your attention to the military where "service" is considered to be a sacrifice, both honorable and heroic, for which a debt of gratitude is expected. And yet, militaries are trained and equipped to kill. That is their mission. And most are good at it.

Therefore, while irrefutably true, there is something equally problematic with fighting, as well as the conditioning that makes it possible. Indoctrinated by their trainers and superiors, a recruit's judgment is deliberately altered while his or her conscience is seared such that they wrongly view those they are ordered to kill as subhuman. Even worse, the public is brainwashed into believing that their freedom and security are provided by these trained killers, their deadly institutions, and vicious weapons.

Further, it is in man's economic systems where most "*'abad* – work" is done. Next time you have a chance, look at your nation's currency. If you are an American, you will see the Eye of Horus, a temple to Ra, and inscriptions promising a New World Order written in the language of Rome, the nation which destroyed Yahowah's Temple and tortured *Dowd* | David when he served as the Passover Lamb.

One more thought before we move on. When we consider the five conditions of the Covenant in light of what Yahowah has told us thus far, there is considerable harmony. To participate in the Covenant, we were asked to walk away from the human schemes born in Babylon and then trust and rely exclusively on Yah, walking to Him while observing His instructions regarding the relationship. And He told us to circumcise our sons so that as fathers we would remember to raise them within the Covenant and not mislead or corrupt them. With this in mind, hasn't God simply reinforced and elaborated upon each of those requests with these statements?

The Creator of the universe and the Author of life does not need to justify His position and explain His overt opposition to us engaging on behalf of religious, political, militaristic, and economic schemes, but He does, nonetheless. Nor is He required to reveal the consequence of such behavior, and yet He does this as well. Listen...

"For, indeed, emphasizing this point, I, Yahowah, your God, am a fiercely protective, steadfastly loyal, and jealous God, a God who is desirous of exclusivity in a deeply devoted relationship.

I actually consider and count the perversity of twisting and distorting and the depravity of perverting and manipulating, deviating from the way, of the fathers upon the children up to the third and the fourth generations of those who shun Me, who are openly hostile and adverse toward Me, who strive maliciously against Me while refusing to engage in a relationship with Me." (*Shemowth* 20:5)

Since Yahowah's presentation has focused on the importance of us engaging in an exclusive relationship with Him, such that we are completely devoid of religious affiliations, it is obvious that *qana'* conveys the idea of "being passionate and zealous." It is addressing the Covenant Family and, thereby, speaks of "jealously protecting those God loves."

But there is another meaning. *Qana'* depicts "paying the price to acquire something valuable." Yahowah personally paid a hellish price to ransom us so that He could reconcile His relationship with us. And in this light, *qana'* speaks of "redemption." It is therefore not unreasonable for God to want to enjoy the company of those He paid to redeem. Likewise, it is wholly appropriate for Yahowah to be exasperated with parents who take their children away from Him – depriving them of what God has gone to such lengths to provide.

I would be remiss as a guide if I did not expose the fact that when Paul wrote of "love" in his first letter to the Corinthians, he lied because he said that "love is not jealous" and that "love does not seek its own." True love is always jealous, and it always seeks to be loved in return. Since no one's love is truer than Yah's, and He is jealous, Paul cannot be trusted.

As was the case previously, there are two verbs in this statement. The first is *paqad* which means "to count or reckon." Written in the qal stem, God isn't kidding. So, while He has chosen to turn a blind eye to the victims of religion and to turn a deaf ear to their prayers, He not only pays attention to those who " *'awon* – twist and distort" His testimony, He keeps a record of their corruptions. And the purpose of doing so is to judge the religious and condemn them with their own words.

Scribed as a participle, *paqad* becomes a verbal adjective, thereby, modifying *'awon* which addresses the "depravity of perverting" God's message and, thereby, "manipulating people so that they miss the way." From this perspective, *paqad*'s other meanings come into play. Those liable for perpetrating *babel* | confounding confusion will be "summoned, judged, and punished" for having committed the most heinous of all crimes. You may rest assured, all religious and most political leaders will be judged and condemned. Their souls will spend an eternity in *She'owl*, more universally known as "Hell." God does not take kindly to deception, and in such matters, He is unforgiving.

There are few if any Hebrew words worse than *'awon*. Derived from *'aw'ah*, it speaks of "distorting, perverting, and warping" and, thus, represents a particular type of sin: *babel*. Affirming this, *'aw'ah* is from *'awah* which is "to bend, twist, and distort." As such, *'awon* depicts "corruption, perversion, distortion, and manipulation" of God's testimony, the very things religious institutions have done to Yah's Towrah teaching, "twisting" His Word so that people "miss the way."

No one was better at this or more influential than Paul, the founder of the Christian religion. His 14 letters routinely remove God's statements from their context, misquote what He said, and then twist the resulting corruption to warp the minds of those who are fooled into believing him. And the consequence has been grievous because, from God's perspective, those who are *'awon* are "perverse, depraved, and reprehensible." It is "wrong."

31

They are "wrong." It is "delusional," as are they. Therefore, "the guilty will be punished for having caused others to deviate" from the truth.

And speaking of truth, there is a sobering aspect of this statement that not one in a million people appreciates. Overtly religious and political parents kill their own children, infecting them with a disease which destroys the souls of their sons and daughters. Raised religious, people stay religious. The child of a Muslim remains a Muslim, just as the child of a Christian stays Christian. *'Awon* fosters a never-ending cycle of death and destruction. It is why 'Abraham was asked to leave *Babel*. It is why God is pleading with us to leave the political and religious aspects of *Babel* | Babylon today.

'Awon is among the worst things a person can do relative to God. He and His Word are one. When you twist His Word, you are attacking Him. And since Yahowah's primary goal is to form a relationship with His creation, by perverting and corrupting His Towrah's Covenant instructions, these people are positioning themselves in direct opposition to Yah's will. Nothing is more hateful because it hampers our ability to know and love Yah.

And that is why the concluding verb, *sane'*, was scribed using the qal stem. The animosity being shown to God is genuine and the opposition toward Him is real. Tell a Christian or Muslim that God's one and only name is Yahowah and see how they react. But it is mutual because scribed as a participle, those who hate Yahowah are despised by Him. Those who are in opposition to God are opposed by God. That certainly seems fair.

We began our review of this, Yahowah's Second of Three introductory Statements, eight pages ago, and yet the most important section remains unexplored. I share this with you because everything we have learned thus far is routinely dismissed by religious Jews and Christians alike

32

with a trite: "Second Commandment: You shall not make an idol."

Now that we know the fate of those who twist Yahowah's testimony, and now that we understand the consequence of doing so with respect to one's children, let's consider the alternative...

"I will genuinely act and actually engage to prepare, perform, and produce unfailing mercy, unearned favor, and genuine kindness, even actual forgiveness, developing a friendly and affectionate relationship on behalf of thousands who move toward Me and love Me, forming a close and familial relationship with Me, caring enough to know Me, approaching Me by closely examining and carefully considering My instructions and directions, the terms and conditions which uphold My Covenant." (*Shemowth* 20:6)

Etched in stone as a qal participle, *'asah* tells us more than just Yahowah "will genuinely act, actually engaging, to literally prepare, perform, and produce" mercy. It reveals that this undeserved favor and unearned kindness is a participatory endeavor. In that *'asah* serves to modify *chesed*, this also means that we have to act and engage to participate in our salvation. That is not to say that we earn it, but only that "*chesed* – mercy" as a relational term requires mutual involvement. This is to say that, to receive God's "*chesed* – favor," we have to act relative to the terms and instructions of His Covenant.

Just as *'awon* is bad, *chesed* is good. Just as Yah is opposed to "*'awon* – corruption," He is the source of "*chesed* – mercy." We are distanced from Him by *'awon*, and we come to Him through *chesed*. One is of man; the other is of God.

Yah's "*chesed* – unearned favor and undeserved kindness" is born out of His zeal for us and His passion for the Covenant relationship. God, Himself, makes this point when He says that He favors those who " *'ahab* – love" Him. In so doing, Yahowah has defined the nature and purpose of His Covenant.

This known, Yahowah's mercy isn't for everyone. Very few are saved. In fact, it is so few that Yah speaks of thousands among billions. And that is just one in a million.

'Eleph is "a cardinal number, an actual mathematical representation, designating one thousand." Emphasizing this point, 500 of the 505 occasions *'eleph* appears in the Torah, Prophets, and Psalms, it is translated as "thousand." Moreover, there is no wiggle room here. *Shemowth* 34:7 and *Dabarym* 5:10 directly affirm this same statement expressly limiting those saved to " *'elephym* – thousands." As a further affirmation of the amount, in *Shemowth* 18:21, *'elephym* is used to convey "thousands" in conjunction with "hundreds" and "tens" in descending order.

Fortunately, God wrote *'elephym*, thereby denoting "thousands," plural and not singular. And while billions and millions are comprised of thousands, Hebrew is fully capable of expressing the concepts of tens of thousands, hundreds of thousands, and even millions and billions, but God did not communicate those numbers here. So, perhaps no fewer than two thousand nor more than twenty thousand souls will be reconciled and thus saved. Of the tens of billions of people who have been born on this planet that is less than one in a million. Most of the rest have been " *'awon* – corrupted" by their parent's *babel*.

As we consider what we must do to get on our Heavenly Father's shortlist, let's examine the verbs which explain how this is done. First, we have *'ahab* which describes the Covenant as "a close, personal, affectionate and loving relationship which is both friendly and familial." God chose to write *'ahab* as a qal participle – communicating something which must be considered genuine and be interpreted literally. Also, as a verbal adjective, there is a demonstrable and vivid influence upon the accompanying nouns which are God and the thousands who reciprocate His love.

Most translators ignore the fact that "'*ahab* – love" was prefixed with the preposition, *la*. In its simplest form, *la* means "to." It denotes "movement toward a goal" which, in this case, is "to approach" Yahowah in love. *La* speaks of "being concerned about someone" and of "being in accord with them."

To my mind, the inclusion of the preposition "*la* – toward" in reference to God, especially in the context of receiving His "*chesed* – unmerited favor," explains God's third requirement for participating in the Covenant. Yah asks us to "walk to Him and become perfect" which is to be considered right and thus innocent. Therefore, three of the five things God asked us to accept if we want to develop a relationship with Him have been scribed by His own hand.

We should not be surprised that the fourth requirement is emblazoned in: "*la shamar mitswah* – approach Me by closely observing, carefully examining, and thoughtfully considering the terms of My relationship agreement." Since the *mitswah* serve as the "terms and conditions, instructions and directions of the Covenant," to *shamar mitswah* is to *shamar beryth*.

Yahowah has used *la* as a prepositional prefix which, when deployed in conjunction with *shamar mitswah*, tells us that His mercy is for those who "approach Him by considering the terms of His Covenant." Further, written in the qal stem, these instructions relative to our salvation are to be interpreted literally. Therefore, if you want to go to heaven, you need to observe the Towrah – the only place where the *mitswah* can be examined and considered. Further, by communicating this as a verbal adjective in the construct form, we learn that God's terms not only influence the observant but, also, that these conditions are absolute and our consideration of them should never cease.

Yahowah has reiterated and explained four of the Covenant's five requirements. And while they have been presented in no uncertain terms, it is possible to derive the fifth condition from this inscription. Yahowah has asked us to circumcise our sons such that we remember to direct their steps toward God and not away from Him. This act, as the sign of the Covenant, demonstrates not only our acceptance of its terms but, also, our willingness to share its benefits with our children so that they grow up to be God's children. I can think of nothing which is more effective in keeping fathers from corrupting their children than this.

Even though God etched this idea in stone, revealing the consequence of misleading our children, we find fathers corrupting His message to the point no child could possibly understand. Consider this…

"Thou shalt not make unto thee any graven image, or any likeness of anything that is in heaven above, or that is in the earth beneath, or that is in the water under the earth. (20:4) Thou shalt not bow down thyself to them, nor serve them: for I the Lord thy God am a jealous God, visiting the iniquity of the fathers upon the children unto the third and fourth generation of them that hate me; (20:5) And shewing mercy unto thousands of them that love me, and keep my commandments." (Exodus 20:6 KJV)

And while that's bad, the Jewish Publication Society is worse, corrupting Exodus 20:6 to read: "and showing mercy unto the thousandth generation of them that love Me and keep My commandments."

𐤋𐤄𐤅𐤄

36

Now that we have seen the Covenant's conditions reaffirmed, let's turn to the Third Statement Yahowah engraved upon the First of these Two Tablets. For all of those who find no issue with ignoring God's name, for those insisting that His name is either unpronounceable or irrelevant, for those who believe that it does not matter what we call God, and for those who protest that God has many names, God begs to differ.

As we approach His next statement, we are confronted with a bit of a challenge – one somewhat compounded by the fact that the Towrah's *Shemowth* / Exodus presentation of what Yahowah wrote on the Tablets is not extant among the Dead Sea Scrolls – although Moseh's recap of them in *Dabarym* / Deuteronomy 5 is available to us for comparison. As such, we are not dependent upon the Masoretic Text for our translation only so far as Shemowth and Dabarym differ. This is relevant because the Masoretic Text was scribed in the 11th century CE by placing diacritical markings on Babylonian Hebrew characters, often changing the meanings of the words they were vocalizing. Otherwise, we would have had no way of effectively arguing that Yahowah may have intended to convey *nasha'* rather than *nasa'*, even though these words would have been written identically in Ancient Hebrew 𐤍𐤔𐤀 and in Babylonian Hebrew נשא.

Today, 3,472 years after these words were originally scribed, and 900 after the Masoretes' intervention, our choice is נָשָׁא versus נָשָׂא (*nasha'* compared to *nasa'* noting the dot over the right and then left side of the middle letter changing a shin into a sin). For reasons only known to these rabbis, the Masoretes invented a second means to denote the "s" sound originally conveyed via a Samech, dividing the Shin into two letters. So, while there was originally no distinction between *nasa'* and *nasha'*, one exists now in the lexicons as a result of a dot added in the 11th century of the common era to either the left שׂ or right שׁ side of the Shin.

37

This is of concern because, by dotting the Shin one way or the other, two words with different meanings have been arbitrarily created out of one by religious clerics. Aware of this, all we can do is set aside their gerrymandering and let the text determine whether Yahowah intended to convey the message of *nasa'*, of *nasha'*, or both. This determination, along with correcting the vocalization of *shav'* to *showa'*, requires our attention because they represent two of the three actionable words in Yah's Third Statement.

Having examined 4QDeut, the oldest surviving parchment attesting to what Yahowah wrote, I can affirm that we are equally justified translating "*lo' nasa'* – you should never lift up or bear" or "*lo' nasha'* – you should never deceive or delude." Therefore, we will proceed using the context of Yah's testimony to guide us, recognizing that the consequences are enormous. Our response to this next statement is life or death and, for many, it may actually be salvation versus damnation. That is because God said that He "will not forgive" anyone who commits the offense presented in what has been mislabeled "The Third Commandment."

With death serving as the consequence and damnation as the potential penalty for failing to observe this Instruction, it is reasonable to conclude that the crime must be serious. And in that light, it is hard to miss the fact that "*lo' nasa'* – you should not lift up or bear" is far less indicting than "*lo' nasha'* – you should not beguile."

Furthermore, as we strive to understand what Yahowah conveyed, it is also important to appreciate that the primary and secondary definitions of *nasa'*, which are "to lift up" and "to bear," are awkward in both sentences which comprise the Third Statement. It is only by extrapolating "lift up" to mean "advance or promote" and "bear" to mean "tolerate or support" that *nasa'* can be construed to fit in either declaration. And since *nasa'*'s

38

tertiary definition is "to forgive," its fourth is "to respect," and its fifth is "to desire," the further we go down the line, the potential for *nasa'* conveying what Yah intended continues to fade.

But that is not the case with *nasha'*, whose primary connotation is "to beguile, to delude, to deceive, and to lead astray." Even the secondary meaning of *nasha'* works effectively in this Statement: "to unfairly enrich oneself by indebting others." These are things God detests because they separate Him from those who would otherwise become His children. *Nasha'* isn't something Yah would be prone to forgive while *nasa'* is something Yah is committed to accomplishing.

Also telling, *nashah,* which would be pronounced identically to *nasha'*, means "to forget or cause to be forgotten," either "failing to properly recall or to make someone forget." In a statement which speaks of eternal damnation for those who act fraudulently with regard to Yahowah's name such that it is forgotten as a result of being edited out of His testimony, this should be alarming. Almost every religious person, alive or deceased, has contributed to this crime by either perpetrating it or by embracing the consequence.

Religious scholars, ignoring everything we have just learned, oblivious as to whether Yah intended to convey the meaning of *nasa'* or *nasha'*, and perhaps to disguise their culpability, reduce this wealth of information down to a single and unjustified word: "take." According to almost every Bible publication: "You shall not *take* the name of the Lord, God, in vain." This, of course, is utterly senseless. You can't "take" the name of God. Yahowah's name is not "Lord." And "vain" speaks of either "failure" or "ego," neither of which apply.

The second verb in the Third Statement is *showa'* 𐤏𐤅𐤔, although you won't find it in any lexicon. It is usually transliterated *shav'* even though that is wrong on three accounts. First, there was no letter or sound "v" in the Hebrew alphabet at this time. The Wah is a vowel, and it conveys either the "o" or the "u" sound. And the concluding Aleph is pronounced "a" or "e." Therefore, the word is most likely *showa'* but with decreasing reliability could be pronounced: *showe', shuwa',* or *shuwe'.* But under no circumstances can Shin-Wah-Aleph be *shav.*

Now that we know the range of permissible pronunciations, our job has only begun. And that is because *showa'* also conveys a range of meanings. *Showa'* speaks of "emptiness and nothingness, worthlessness and failure, lying and falsehood" as well as "deception, idolatry, and futility." The effect of *showa'* is to be "ravaged, devastated, ruined, and laid waste, to be hastily rushed over and hostilely trodden down, leaving only lifelessness and desolation." *Showa'* is the epitome of "horribly mistreating someone."

Especially germane in the context of deceiving in association with His name, Yahowah, and replacing it with "the Lord," the unforgivable sin associated with *showa'* is "negating the value of" God's name by deceptively "removing it," such that it "no longer exists" in the text of His testimony. Discounting all of this, or perhaps oblivious to it, almost every English Bible distills *showa'* down to "in vain." And while "vain" does convey "failure," the Hebrew preposition *ba*, denoting "in," is not "*ba* – in" either sentence.

All of these things known, and after considerable research and contemplation, I have decided to base the following translation upon *nasha'* while still reflecting the insights *nasa'* provides. Further, since it is safer to provide too much information rather than too little, you will find that the cause and effect of *showa'* have been blended into both sentences, emphasizing different aspects in each of its two appearances. I suspect that God repeated both words to provide us with the unique opportunity to consider every aspect of each term expressly because He does not want us to be among those who are "*lo' naqah* – not forgiven."

Therefore, without further ado, here then is the Third and final Statement Yahowah engraved on the First of Two Tablets:

"You should not continue to deceive, nor should you tolerate or support delusions (*lo' nasha'* – you should not habitually deploy or advance clever tricks to enrich yourself by indebting others, and should avoid actually beguiling people on an ongoing basis by consistently lifting up, promoting, or forgiving that which causes them to miss the way by forgetting that which is (qal imperfect)) **associated with** (*'eth* – through or by way of the) **the name and reputation** (*shem* – the renown and proper designation) **of Yahowah** (*YaHoWaH* – an accurate presentation of the name of *'elowah* – God as guided by His *towrah* – instructions regarding His *hayah* – existence), **your God** (*'elohym*), **thereby advancing worthless and lifeless deceptions** (*la ha showa'* (errantly transliterated *shav'*) – deploying that which advances devastating dishonesty, nullifying one's existence, leading to emptiness and nothingness, so as to advance deceitful and lifeless lies which are ineffectual, futile, and ruinous).

For, indeed (*ky* – because), **Yahowah** (*YaHoWaH* – an accurate presentation of the name of *'elowah* – God as guided by His *towrah* – instructions regarding His *hayah* – existence) **will not forgive or leave unpunished** (*lo' naqah* – as an ongoing admonition unconstrained by time, He will not purify or pardon, He will not acquit or free from guilt, He will not exempt from judgment or sentencing, nor will He consider innocent or release (piel imperfect)) **those who** (*'eth 'asher* – in association with others) **consistently deceive, actually beguile, and habitually delude, promote or accept trickery so as to forget** (*nasha'* – religiously using deception to continually mislead, lifting

41

up and advancing a clever, albeit dishonest, ruse (qal imperfect)) **in association with** (*'eth* – through) **His name** (*shem* – renown, reputation, and proper designation) **to advance and promote** (*la* – to bring into effect accordingly) **vain and ineffectual lies which lead to lifelessness, nullifying one's existence** (*showa'* – devastating deceptions which destroy, leading to emptiness, worthlessness, and nothingness, futilely deceiving in a ruinous manner)."** (*Shemowth* / Names / Exodus 20:7)

Regardless of how we pronounce or translate the words Yahowah inscribed, God will not forgive those who deceive others – especially when they do so by negating His name or nullifying His reputation. And that means the world's most infamous religious and political leaders, Rabbi Akiba, the wannabe-Apostle Paul, Emperor Hadrian, and the joke-of-a-Prophet Muhammad, will all be spending time together with Satan, the spirit they served – although I don't suspect they will enjoy it very much.

There is only one thing Yahowah hates more than deadly and beguiling deceptions, and that is when they are promoted by those who claim to be speaking for Him. Therefore, when it comes to judgment, you don't want to be in the same line as the popes, imams, monks, sheiks, rabbis, or philosophers.

But here is the silver lining: Since every verb was presented in the imperfect, which speaks of that which is continuous and ongoing, with the negation *lo'* provides, rather than simply saying, "You should not," or worse, "You should never," it is more accurate to say, "Do not make a practice of deception..." This perspective is further developed by the qal stem which, in addition to requiring a literal interpretation, conveys a sense of authenticity, sincerity, and genuineness.

Also interesting, God hasn't written anything on the First of these Two Tablets using the imperative mood, which is the only form of Hebrew grammar where the opportunity exists to render a statement as a command. Although, as we have noted, the imperative is most often used to convey an exhortation which is subject to second-person volition. As such, there have not been any "Commandments" communicated thus far. Instead, these Instructions are as Yahowah wrote: "*dabar* – Statements" composed of "*dabarym* – Words." God is providing direction. He is guiding us, attempting to teach us so that we come to know and to understand how to properly respond to Him.

Contrary to more popular translations, God was not so trivial or vain that He asked us not to swear, or say "God Damn," as Christians would have you believe. Knowing and using Yahowah's name is essential to our relationship and salvation, and yet there is not a single significant religious institution on Earth proclaiming it. Indeed, most hide it or deny it, removing it from their Bibles and Talmuds, sermons and synagogues.

As a result, Yahowah is being merciful and compassionate by revealing that He is intolerant of lies and deceptions, as well as of empty religious promises. This is especially true when they negate the importance of His name. Nothing is more destructive, deadly, or damning.

There is something else here we ought not miss. Yahowah just said that those who "*nasha'* – deceive" in association with His "*shem* – name" will "*lo' naqah* – not be forgiven or left unpunished." And while not being pardoned by God equates to death and to the destruction of a person's soul, being sentenced and punished by God is nothing short of eternal damnation.

As you continue to read these books you will discover that there are three, not two, destinations for human souls.

Most souls simply cease to exist at the end of their mortal life and are neither punished nor rewarded as a result. If you or someone you know is an outspoken advocate, apologist, evangelist, propagandist, or jihadist for any religion, regardless of whether it is Judaism, Christianity, Islam, or Socialist Secular Humanism, it is best that their soul ceases and desists. Death is infinitely better than damnation, and now we and they have been warned.

Also, *lo' naqah* was scribed in the piel imperfect. The piel stem reveals that those who deceive will bring judgment upon themselves. Someone who is a religious apostle, evangelist, or apologist, even a political activist, strategist, or propagandist, is writing their own summons to appear before an unforgiving Judge. Further, in the imperfect, Yahowah is on record as saying that this was, is, and always will be His policy relative to those who promote delusions in association with His name or reputation.

The First of the Two Tablets is now complete. God has provided us with the vantage point required to facilitate our understanding of His revelation. He has introduced Himself by name. He has told us that His written Word provides the perspective we need to appreciate the role He personally played in rescuing us from the crucible of judgment and oppressive political and religious schemes. And He revealed that we will cease to exist if we continue to worship gods of our own making.

Yah said that He is opposed to religious rituals, to religious rhetoric, to religious art, to religious statuary, icons, and imagery. He wants us to disassociate ourselves and walk away from these things. He has stated that He is passionate about our relationship with Him. He wants it to be exclusive – without a rival. He does not want us to corrupt our children by twisting His testimony. And His mercy is for those who approach Him, walking to Him in love, by observing His instructions.

By telling us that He would hold those hostile to Him accountable for the perverse act of twisting and manipulating His message, fraudulently removing His name and unconscionably replacing "Yahowah" with "the Lord," God not only affirmed that many would indeed distort and pervert His testimony, editing His words to their liking but also that our children would be victimized by society's willingness to deviate from His Way in this way.

Having reiterated, affirmed, and explained all five of the Covenant's conditions, Yahowah's written testimony leaves us without excuse. He has tried to direct our steps and to guide us from this world to His home.

Yahowah has also undermined every popular religious scheme. God declared that He would personally prepare, perform, and produce unearned favor and unfailing mercy on behalf of thousands, not millions or billions, and only for those who approach Him in love and who closely observe and carefully consider these Instructions. This means that the Savior is Yahowah, Himself, and that just one in a million people will avail themselves of His generosity.

Further, Yahowah's provision is for those who rely upon Him, who have come to love Him and His "*shem –* personal and proper name.*" But more than this, they have all approached God by closely observing and carefully considering His Directions – all of which are enshrined in this very same Towrah. He has delineated the way home, providing the path to eternal life in heaven.

And yet, God's Way, the path where our devotion is directed toward the Author of the Towrah, the plan where we are asked to observe all that He spoke through His prophets, is in direct conflict with the notions prescribed by Christians, Jews, and Muslims – as well as the way of multiculturalism and political correctness, especially those lost in the contrived world of being woke and progressive.

For some, the arrogance behind the crime of deliberately and unconscionably removing Yahowah's name from the text He inspired, and then replacing YaHoWaH with the title "Lord," was reason enough to leave church and synagogue. If the religious scholars and clerics, priests and pastors, in addition to rabbis, along with the institutions they represent, were willing to perpetrate this act of thievery and then support the deception, why would anyone trust them or their religion?

Few statements have been as inadequately and errantly translated as those that Yahowah wrote on this Tablet. Ironically, the convoluted and twisted biblical renditions of these Statements serve to prove the validity of Yahowah's prediction that men would corrupt His Word. But knowing that many would do this very thing in the names of their religions, Yahowah warned those who mislead, promoting ineffectual lifeless and destructive lies, that He would not forgive them and would punish them. And that, my friends, will make "Hell" a very religious place.

Following this introduction, the First Tablet Yahowah etched in stone reads:

"Then, Almighty God conveyed, communicating by enabling and empowering all of these statements comprised of words in our presence, providing perspective, saying and explaining: (*Shemowth* 20:1)

'I am Yahowah, your God (a ram among the sheep and your shepherd, your doorway to an expansive and abundant life) who, to show the correct path to get the most out of life, brought you out and delivered you, descending to serve you by doing everything which was required to lead those who respond away from the crucibles of political, religious, economic, and military oppression, out of the house of slavery, the place of worship and servitude, of bondage and working for

46

one's salvation, and of man's authority. (*Shemowth* 20:2)

You shall not continue to exist with other, different or additional, gods over and above My presence. (*Shemowth* 20:3)

You should not continue to associate yourself with or make a practice of attending to, you should not act upon or engage on behalf of a religious image, an object of worship, or any representation of a god, even a picture or painting depicting that which is in the heavens above, including the sun, moon, planets, and stars, or which is on the earth below, even that which is in the waters beneath the land. (*Shemowth* 20:4)

You should not speak about them on your own initiative or make a practice of bowing down and worshiping them, you should not continue to promote their message on your own accord or display their words because such uncoerced and ongoing verbal declarations will influence you, nor should you habitually worship them, especially if not compelled or forced, and you should not serve them or coerce anyone to be passionate about them. Do not continually work or labor in their cause nor make a career of serving as their ministers, nor encourage anyone else to do so.

For, indeed, emphasizing this point, I, Yahowah, your God, am a fiercely protective, steadfastly loyal, and jealous God, a God who is desirous of exclusivity in a deeply devoted relationship.

I actually consider and count the perversity of twisting and distorting and the depravity of perverting and manipulating, deviating from the way, of the fathers upon the children up to the third and the fourth generations of those who shun Me, who are openly hostile and adverse toward Me, who strive maliciously against Me while refusing to engage in a relationship with Me. (*Shemowth* 20:5)

I will genuinely act and actually engage to prepare, perform, and produce unfailing mercy, unearned favor, and genuine kindness, even actual forgiveness, developing a friendly and affectionate relationship on behalf of thousands who move toward Me and love Me, forming a close and familial relationship with Me, caring enough to know Me, approaching Me by closely examining and carefully considering My instructions and directions, the terms and conditions which uphold My Covenant. (*Shemowth* 20:6)

You should not continue to deceive, nor should you tolerate or support delusions, you should not habitually deploy or advance clever tricks to enrich oneself by indebting others and should avoid actually beguiling people so that they forget by consistently lifting up, promoting, or forgiving that which causes them to miss the way associated with the name and reputation of Yahowah, your God, thereby advancing worthless and lifeless deceptions, deploying that which condones devastating dishonesty, nullifying one's existence.

For, indeed, Yahowah will not forgive or leave unpunished, He will not pardon or acquit, freeing from guilt or exempting from either judgment or sentencing, nor will He consider an individual innocent nor release those who consistently deceive, who actually beguile and habitually delude, promote or accept trickery, using religious duplicity to mislead, lifting up or advancing a clever, albeit dishonest, ruse to forget His name and proper designation to bring into effect vain and ineffectual lies which lead to lifelessness, nullifying one's existence.'" (*Shemowth* / Names / Exodus 20:7)

𐤉𐤄𐤅𐤄

2

Mala'kah | Spiritual Counselor

Instructions…

What follows is a treatise on the Sabbath, on our relationship with our Heavenly Father and Spiritual Mother as well as how to behave spiritually and morally. On the Second of the Two Tablets Yahowah wrote the following Seven Instructions beginning with:

"**Remember** (*zakar* – actually recall, bring to mind and genuinely reflect upon, recognize and mention, be reminded of and proclaim, earnestly and intensely memorializing (qal infinitive absolute)) **that the Shabat** (*'eth ha shabat* – that this, the seventh day, the period of reflecting on the relationship at the end of the week, reminiscent of the promise of settling debts so we can settle down by observing the oath of association; from *shaba'* – fulfilling and satisfying the promise of seven to abundantly empower and enrich) **day** (*yowm* – time) **is set apart to approach Him** (*la qadash* – is separated unto Him for purifying and cleansing and thus special to Him (piel stem – where the object, Yahowah, is engaged and acts in response to the subject's (our) willingness to set this day apart and infinitive construct – serving as a verbal noun)). (*Shemowth* / Names / Exodus 20:8)

Six (*shesh* – speaking of that which is bleached white or adorned in fine linen (also the number of man created on the sixth)) **days** (*yowmym* – periods of time) **you should actually and continuously work** (*'abad* – you should engage in ongoing labor, working for oneself or another, expending the energy to be productive at your job (qal stem – denoting a literal interpretation and imperfect conjugation – which speaks of that which is ongoing)), **and** (*wa*) **choose to act upon while time permits, genuinely engaging in** (*'asah* – express your own freewill to prepare and accomplish what you can do at this time, capitalizing upon and advancing, doing and profiting from this brief moment from (qal stem – addresses genuine relationships, perfect conjugation – denoting actions which are complete and have been accomplished at some point in time, and consecutive mood – conveying volition)) **all** (*kol* – the entirety of) **your service with the Spiritual Messenger** (*Mala'kah 'atah* – your usefulness communicating on behalf of the Maternal Heavenly Representative, working alongside the Spiritual Counselor, making informative announcements on behalf of God's envoy; the feminine singular form of *mal'ak* – the maternal representation of God's message and spirituality, serving humankind as a heavenly representative dispatched to inform, protect, and guide). (*Shemowth* / Exodus 20:9)

But (*wa*) **the seventh** (*shaby'iy* – the solemn promise which fulfills and satisfies, abundantly enriching those who listen and are observant of the role of the seven; from *shaba'* – to take an oath and make a sworn promise to fulfill, completely satisfying, providing an abundance of enriching benefits) **day** (*yowm* – period of time)**, the Shabat** (*'eth ha shabat* – the seventh day, the period of reflecting on the relationship at the end of the week, reminiscent of the promise of settling debts so we can settle down by observing the oath of association; from *shaba'* – fulfilling and satisfying the promise of seven to abundantly empower and enrich) **is to approach** (*la* – is for drawing near, associating with and moving toward) **Yahowah** (*Yahowah* – a transliteration of 𐤉𐤄𐤅𐤄, our *'elowah* – God as directed in His *towrah* – teaching regarding His *hayah* – existence), **your God** (*'elohym 'atah*).

You should not continuously engage in (*lo' 'asah* – you should not habitually act out, consistently preparing or producing, nor should you try to actually fashion, accomplish, or constantly do (qal stem imperfect conjugation)) **all of** (*kol*) **the work of the Maternal Counselor and Spiritual Messenger** (*Mala'kah* – service of the Heavenly Envoy; feminine singular of *mal'ak* – the ministry and mission of the Spiritual Envoy, the labor of God's maternal manifestation and presence) **yourself** (*'atah*)**, your son** (*ben*)**, your daughter** (*bat*)**, your male and female servants and staff** (*'ebed wa 'amah* – your employees and those men and women who work for and with you)**, your means of production** (*bahemah* – your animals and beasts of burden) **as well as** (*wa*) **those visitors** (*ger* – foreigners) **who relationally** (*'asher*) **are in your home or on your property** (*ba sha'ar* – are inside your doors or gates; from *sha'ar* – to think and be reasonable)**.** (*Shemowth* / Exodus 20:10)

For, indeed (*ky* – because)**, in six** (*shesh* – symbolic of mankind being bleached white and purified on the sixth) **days** (*yowmym*)**, Yahowah** (*Yahowah* – God's name transliterated as guided by His *towrah* – instructions on His *hayah* – existence and His role in our *shalowm* – reconciliation as *'elowah* – Almighty God) **acted and engaged, preparing and producing everything associated with completing** (*'asah* – totally fashioning, instituting, advancing, accomplishing, doing, celebrating, and attending to the full extent of (qal stem perfect conjugation)) **the heavens** (*'eth ha shamaym* – the spiritual realm)**, and the earth** (*wa ha 'erets* – the material world)**, and the waters** (*wa ha yam*)**, and all** (*kol* – everything) **which relationally** (*'asher*) **is in them** (*ba hem*).

Then (*wa*)**, He became completely settled spiritually** (*nuwach* – He was satisfied after settling all unresolved issues by way of the Spirit (*nuwach* is related to *ruwach* – spirit)) **during** (*ba*) **the Almighty's seventh** (*ha shaby'iy 'al* – God's solemn promise which fulfills and satisfies those who listen and are observant of the role of the oath of the seventh) **day** (*yowm*).

Therefore (*ken* – consequently, this is true and correct), **Yahowah** (*YaHoWaH* – an accurate presentation of the name of *'elowah* – God as guided by His *towrah* – instructions regarding His *hayah* – existence) **blessed and adored** (*barak* – knelt down and lowered Himself, offering a greeting along with an opportunity to meet, favoring (piel perfect)) **everything associated with this day** (*'eth ha yowm*), **the Shabat** (*'eth ha shabat* – the seventh day, the period of reflection at the end of the week, reminiscent of the promise of settling debts so we can settle down by observing the oath in association with this means to satisfy and enrich), **setting it apart** (*qodesh* – separating it from that which is common, ordinary, and popular, making it special, dedicating it to separation, cleansing, and purifying)." (*Shemowth* / Names / Exodus 20:11)

This is one of the rare incidences where the title Shabat is considerably more important than the verbal form of the word, especially in Yah's lexicon. Therefore, we should rightly question whether the "rest and reflect, cease and desist" connotations of the verb *shabath* apply to the noun. If so, in addition to taking the day off from your job, we should strive to be inactive. If not, we should focus on the insights we can glean from *shaba'*, the root of *shabat*, which means both "promise" and "seven," to "fulfill" and "satisfy," even "abundantly enrich."

In this light, as we consider the role of the Shabat during the *Miqra'ey* | Invitations to be Called Out and Meet with God, we will discover that *Shabat* is routinely used as a verbal noun. And this means that the Shabat must be actionable and thus active. In the single most identifying and controlling aspect of Judaism, the Shabat, the religious have it wrong. They have conjured a thousand ways to do nothing and haven't a clue as to how to properly celebrate the Covenant relationship.

We have been asked to follow Yahowah's example, enjoying the seventh day by remembering to reflect upon the promise He has made to us, and subsequently fulfilled, to settle our debts. Since God, in conjunction with His Son and the Set-Apart Spirit, has resolved every issue which would otherwise separate us, it is appropriate that we do not attempt to replicate what they have already accomplished and fulfilled. Considering the magnitude of what occurred on the Shabat of UnYeasted Bread in 33 CE so that we might enjoy being among the *Bikuwrym* / Firstborn Children the following day, it is not too much to ask.

While a superficial reading of this instruction seems to ask that we refrain from working on the Shabat, the deeper spiritual message is that Yahowah has promised to bring us into His home and save us so long as we rely on Him to do His job. And that is why Yahowah told us that "the Shabat day is set apart to approach Him."

There are some essential aspects of *qodesh* which are seldom considered. And this is because English Bibles routinely ascribe the religious concept of "sacred" or worse, "holy," to *qodesh*, thereby misleading believers.

First, *qodesh* affirms that the Shabat (it can also be transliterated as Shabath) is "set apart." "Set apart from what?" is the obvious question. The answer is that it is separate and distinct from the common things of man such as religion and politics, militarism and economics, conspiracy and culture. This is important because the purpose of the Covenant is to set us apart from mankind's corruptions, from death and destruction, and unto God.

Therefore, the Shabat is the antithesis of anything which is popular or ordinary such as religious beliefs, national politics, shows of patriotism, economic activity, military endeavors, societal customs, and the promotion of conspiracies. *Qodesh* thereby encourages us to distance ourselves from all of these things. And in this regard, Yahowah is reiterating essential aspects of the requirements to participate in His Covenant.

Second, the *Ruwach Qodesh* is the Set-Apart Spirit, the Maternal aspect of Yahowah's nature. *Qodesh* makes us aware that the Spirit is part of Yahowah, set apart from Him.

The third seldom considered benefit of the Shabat is directly related to the previous two. *Qodesh* reveals that it "serves to cleanse and purify us" from the corrupt and pervasive nature of religion so that we can approach Yahowah.

As with almost everything Yahowah reveals, there is more to the First of Seven Instructions God etched in stone on how to live our lives than initially meets the eye. In this regard, the Shabat is about "*nuwach* – relying upon the Spirit" because God wants us to realize the role He plays in our salvation. While we must act and engage to benefit, it is His actions which make the advantages possible.

Yahowah accomplishes this merciful result by way of "*nuwach* – spiritually settling and satisfying" our debts so that, "reconciled," we might become "*qodesh* – set apart" unto Him. This, in turn, enables our Heavenly Father to "*nuwach* – settle us spiritually" in His home. This is among the reasons everything which is important to God is "*qodesh* – set apart," including the *Shabat* and *Miqra'ey*, *Ruwach Qodesh*, the Towrah and its Covenant, Yisra'el and Yahuwdah.

When it comes to our existence, and to life itself, God has a plan, one which He has and will continue to follow, and one which He wants us to understand. It is based upon six, which is symbolic of man, who was created on the sixth day, in addition to God, who is one, equaling the perfect result, represented by the promise of seven. For example, there are seven Invitations to be Called Out and Meet with

God, six steps we must follow to enter God's home: Passover, UnYeasted Bread, Firstborn Children, the Promise of Seven, Trumpets, and Reconciliations. Collectively, these six steps lead to Shelters, the seventh Festival Feast, where we camp out with our Heavenly Father.

And lest we forget, by proclaiming the importance of observing the Shabat, God has once again placed Himself in conflict with the world's two most popular religions: Islam and Christianity whose adherents pray and worship on Friday and Sunday. So, I ask you: why do you suppose the founders of these religions collectively thumbed their noses at God's instructions by selecting days on either side of the Shabat? The answer, while unpopular, is obvious: Muhammad and Paul were so opposed to God that they routinely contradicted Him.

Do not be swayed by the Christian myth that we "should worship God every day, making Sunday as good as any other." God not only does not want to be worshiped, there is but one day, at the exclusion of all others, set apart to focus on our relationship with Him. The Babylonians, Assyrians, Egyptians, Greeks, and Romans worshiped their sun gods on Sunday which is why Sunday Worship and Easter Sunday were mandated by the Roman Catholic Church in direct conflict with Yahowah's instructions. There is absolutely no justification for either in any of the words Yahowah inspired men to scribe on our behalf.

But this leads to another question: do the billions of Muslims and Christians who thoughtlessly rush into mosques and churches on Fridays and Sundays without resolving this conflict believe God is capricious (and thus unreliable) or that God has given religious clerics the authority to contradict Him? Or has their faith preempted thinking?

Additional insights can be gleaned by those who go back in time and view the picture painted by the Ancient-Hebrew alphabet with which these instructions were originally inscribed. *Shabat*, written as שַׁבָּת by the Masoretes, and as ‏ⴕⵎⵞⵞ‏ by Moseh, begins with the letter, ⵞⵞ Shin. It was represented pictorially by teeth and symbolized language and words, instructions and directions, biting and, thus, separation in addition to nourishment. Affirming the central aspects of this legacy, "*shama'* – listen" and "*shamar* – observe" both begin with the letter, Shin.

The second letter, ⵞ Beyth, was depicted by a graphic representation of a sheltered enclosure or dwelling place. It symbolized being part of a family protected inside of a home. Even today, *beyth* means "family and home," and *beryth*, which is derived from it, is the title of Yahowah's "Family-Oriented Covenant Relationship."

The final letter in *shabat*, ✝ Taw, was conveyed in Ancient Hebrew using an upright pillar with a horizontal support beam. It conveyed the idea of supporting and enlarging a tent, especially the Tabernacle, and of posting a sign. It also represented a doorway in addition to a mark, a signpost, and a signature. And since the Taw and Theth were once indistinguishable, if the final letter was written originally as a ⊗ Theth, Yah's Shabat promise unequivocally bears His signature – His mark and sign placed inside of a protective enclosure. Therefore, the letters which form *shabat* convey instructions regarding the doorway which provides access to God's home, to being part of His Family, to bearing His signature and to being sheltered and protected.

Looking even more closely, there is a subtlety with potentially profound implications provided by the imperfect conjugation applied to "*'abad* – work and labor," making it ongoing. Then with the perfect conjugation shading the meaning of "*'asah* – act and engage," this becomes a completed action. Yahowah has no issue with us "continuing to work" on behalf of our families on our time – six days a week. But He wants us to recognize that, once we "act upon the totality" of His Shabat promise, "nothing more needs be done." Once we "embrace" the work of Dowd's soul and the work of the Set-Apart Spirit (especially on Pesach and the Shabat of Matsah), our debts are completely and totally settled. And that is why 'asah is the only volitional verb scribed on these tablets. Relying upon God's service is subject to our freewill. We can choose to be religious and forego access to this relationship – albeit not the brightest of choices.

The idea of Yahowah working with His Son to settle our debts is reinforced by barak in the concluding line. On the Shabat of UnYeasted Bread, Dowd's soul entered She'owl to favor us in the most courageous expression of true love. Acceptance of his sacrifice is what sets us apart from the corrupting ways of man.

In that we have already addressed the fact that these Ten Statements are recorded in Dabarym / Deuteronomy 5 in addition to Shemowth / Exodus 20, there is a remarkable insight in Moseh's presentation of what he saw God write. Dabarym 5:15 reveals: **"You should remember that you were a slave in the land of Egypt and Yahowah, your God, brought you out with a mighty hand, by an outstretched strong arm, with a protective shepherd, and by way of the sacrificial lamb; therefore, Yahowah, your God, appointed and instructed you to act upon and engage in the Shabat day."**

This is interesting because it gives us something profoundly important to think about on this day – and that would be Yahowah's instructions regarding walking away from the crucibles of religion and government, military and economic oppression, and how this principle is manifest throughout the Miqra'ey. But it also reveals that Passover was observed beginning on what we now call a Thursday evening in Mitsraym, just after sunset. Then right after midnight, Pharaoh, after losing his firstborn son, sent the Yisra'elites away in great haste – affirming that the long walk away from dying in Mitsraym to living in Yisra'el began before the sun rose in the early morning hours of what we would now call Friday, such that by sundown at the end of the day, they could observe Matsah on a Shabat – celebrating their newfound freedom. It also means that the Children of Yisra'el spent the Shabat of the Exodus with Yahowah walking away from slavery. And that not only negates the notion of inactivity on this day, but it also reveals that we can spend this day walking with our Heavenly Father.

This is the same weekly sequence that played out in 33 CE when Dowd fulfilled the promise of the Pesach Lamb. His body had served its purpose, Dowd's soul was free to enable the perfecting result of UnYeasted Bread on the Shabat. As a result, we can conclude that Yahowah wants us to see Him as He is, as the Savior and Liberator of those who engage and act upon His instructions.

Therefore, not only does the sequence of days match between the physical enactment and the spiritual fulfillment of Pesach, with Matsah falling on a Shabat, we now have a direct correlation between the Shabat and walking away from all forms of human subjugation. In addition, this expanded presentation of the First Instruction on the Second Tablet serves to correlate the Shabat with the Miqra'ey. Now, there is something to rest and reflect upon!

Since Yahowah provided such a wealth of Instruction regarding the Seventh Day, let's review His guidance before we press on…

"Remember and genuinely reflect upon, recognizing that the Sabbath, which is the seventh day, is set apart to approach Him.

58

Six days you should actually and continuously work, laboring for oneself or another, expending the energy to be productive at your job, and then choose to act upon while time permits, all of your service communicating with the Spiritual Messenger and Heavenly Counselor.

But the seventh, representing the solemn promise which fulfills and satisfies, abundantly enriching those who listen and are observant on this day, the Shabat, the period of reflection at the end of the week, is to approach Yahowah, your God.

You should not continuously engage in all of the work of the *Mala'kah* | God's Heavenly Representative and Spiritual Messenger, yourself, your son, your daughter, your male and female servants and staff, your means of production, as well as those visitors who relationally are in your home or on your property.

For indeed, in six days, Yahowah acted and engaged, preparing and producing everything associated with completing, celebrating and attending to the full extent of the heavens, including the spiritual realm, and the earth, along with the entire material world, even the waters, and all which relationally is in them.

Then, He became completely settled spiritually during the Almighty's seventh day. Therefore, Yahowah blessed and adored, offered a greeting along with an opportunity to meet, favoring everything associated with this day, the Shabat, setting it apart, separating it from that which is common, ordinary, and popular, making it special." (*Shemowth* / Names / Exodus 20:8-11)

𐤋𐤅𐤄𐤅

Having considered the First of the Seven Instructions God etched in stone, we find that the Six which follow are ordered according to their significance. This realization is suggested by the very next word God wrote: *kabed* – meaning "significance." The Hebrew verb, which is habitually translated as "honor" in the context of this instruction, literally means "heavy or weighty." And yet, while *kabed* and its derivatives appear many times in the Towrah, Prophets, and Psalms, there are only two passages, both in Shamuw'el, where it can be translated as such.

On all other occasions, we must render *kabed* symbolically using phrases such as: "very significant, awesomely impressive, great, massive, enormous, valuable, beneficial, worthy of respect, honorable, or weighty in the sense of something which is especially important to consider carefully." Therefore, with *kabed*, we are being alerted not only to the relative significance of the following Instruction but, also, to God's proclivity for symbolism.

From this perspective, the Second of Seven Instructions provides the following spiritual insights:

"You should choose to carefully consider, view as worthy, enormously valuable, extremely significant, and highly enriching (*kabed* – of your own volition elect to distinguish, respect, esteem, and honor, perceiving as awesomely impressive, tremendously relevant, extremely great, and extraordinarily important, even glorious so as to be abundantly enriched and empowered to a very high degree (written in the piel stem revealing that our Heavenly Father and Spiritual Mother are influenced by and respond to our perceptions of them, and in the imperative mood which expresses either a command, an intent, or an exhortation in the second person which is subject to volition)) **accordingly the symbolism of** (*'eth* – that which is represented by and in accord with; from *'owth* – as a miraculous sign and distinguishing symbol based upon your consent to an agreement with) **your Father** (*'ab* – biological, adoptive, or heavenly father) **and** (*wa*) **that which is represented by your** (*'eth* – that which is represented by and in accord with; from *'owth* – as a miraculous sign and distinguishing symbol based upon your consent to an agreement with) **Mother** (*'em* – biological, adoptive, or spiritual mother) **for the purpose of** (*lama'an* – for the intent and sake of, in view and account of, and in order to achieve) **continuously lengthening** (*'arak* – enabling My desire to elongate and always prolong, growing and continuing (written in the hifil stem, imperfect conjugation, and paragogic nun ending which, like the cohortative, expresses volition in the first person)) **your days** (*yowmym 'atah*) **upon** (*'al* – on the) **the land** (*ha 'adamah* – the ground or earth; feminine of *'adam* the name of the first man created in God's image with a *neshamah* – conscience) **which relationally and as a blessing** (*'asher* – to reveal the narrow, correct, beneficial, joyful, and straightforward steps to walk along the path to get the most out of life) **Yahowah** (*Yahowah* – the proper pronunciation of YaHoWaH, our *'elowah* – God as directed in His *ToWRaH* – teaching regarding His *HaYaH* – existence and our *ShaLoWM* – restoration)**, your God** (*'elohym 'atah*)**, is actually giving to you** (*nathan la 'atah* – is literally producing, providing, allowing, granting, and genuinely bestowing to you as a gift and for you to approach and draw near (qal participle))**."** (*Shemowth* / Names / Exodus 20:12)

Reinforcing the realization that this Instruction differs from the four statements which have preceded it, this is the first and only time one of the verbs Yahowah etched in stone was scribed in the imperative mood. It thereby sets the guidance God is providing apart from the other things He has conveyed. By using the imperative, our Heavenly Father revealed that He wants us to exercise our own freewill and choose of our own accord to engage in a family-oriented relationship with He and His *Mala'kah* |

Spiritual Counselor – the *Ruwach Qodesh* | Set-Apart Spirit who is our Heavenly Mother.

The imperative mood is the only form of Hebrew grammar capable of expressing a command – although it more typically conveys an intent or exhortation because it is the mood of volition – conveying the freedom to choose in the second person. And that means that while this, the Fifth of the Ten Statements Yahowah wrote upon the Two Tablets is the only one with even the potential to be considered a "commandment," it is actually the one most subject to freewill. By using the imperative mood in association with *kabed*, Yahowah is "encouraging us to choose to value and respect" the familial nature of His Covenant. It is His desire, but it is our choice. It is His intent, but the option is all ours.

There is nothing more fundamental to the Covenant than a child's relationship with his or her parents. And it is from this perspective that the Covenant is properly understood.

In this statement about our Father and Mother, the supposed "Commandment" least comfortable being rendered as a command, Yahowah interjects His role as Father, the Spirit's role as Mother, and our role as children in His Family-Oriented Covenant Relationship. Among the countless reasons to fall in love with Yah, this may not be leading the parade, but the way this is worded is nonetheless an important part of the chorus. Sure, it is a subtle thing, but so are many of the best things in life.

But that is not the end of the grammatical treasures. The second verb, "*'arak* – to lengthen" which conveys the "*lama'an* – purpose" of "*kabed* – choosing to consider and respect" our Father and Mother, was presented using the hifil stem. This means that the subjects of the verb, our Heavenly Father and Spiritual Mother, cause the object, "*yowm* – our days," to participate in the action – prolonging them – as a secondary subject. Or more simply stated: When we revere and respect, properly valuing our Heavenly Father and Spiritual Mother, we are afforded an elongation of days and, thus, eternal life.

Reinforcing this, Yahowah presented *'arak* using the paragogic nun which, like the cohortative, is a first-person expression of volition. This tells us that it is God's desire that we choose to value our Heavenly Father and Spiritual Mother because this enables Him to do what He wants, which is to lengthen our days – making us eternal. But while it is His intent for us to view our participation in the Covenant this way, the choice which facilitates our adoption is ours. That is the essence of Yahowah expressing His will while not imposing it.

Even more than this, the hifil stem suggests that eternal life is a derivative or subset of God's nature, intent, and purpose. This thereby connects Yahowah to life, and life to the Covenant, while revealing that choice is the avenue to both.

All of this prompts us to consider the prime directive – the Covenant – from God's perspective. He would find no pleasure in extending the lives of those who find no pleasure in spending eternity with Him. An extension of life must be a byproduct of the relationship. It is the Covenant first, salvation second. We must first come to know Yahowah and understand what He wants. If we find Him desirable and His Covenant acceptable then, and only then, should we embrace it.

Since Yahowah etched *'arak* in stone using the imperfect conjugation, we discover that the "lengthening and prolonging" is not finite but is, instead, infinite – unfolding throughout time. The effects are ongoing and continuous throughout the whole fabric of time. And that means God is speaking of eternal life.

Recognizing that these instructions are listed in order of their relevance, and that *kabed* is, in itself, a symbolic term, as is *'eth* (the contracted form of *'owth* which is the Hebrew word for symbolism), this is one of many times where we are actually compelled to consider a verse metaphorically – making this Instruction an especially relevant one to analyze at this juncture.

As we dive deeper into this Instruction, seeking to understand it, remember that on the First Tablet Yahowah wrote that fathers would bring harm upon their own children by corrupting His testimony. Therefore, "carefully considering and respecting" what one's human parents have to say would be counterproductive in this context.

Further, our biological parents are seldom "awesomely important" or "enormously great," and never "glorious." Moreover, it would be extraordinarily unlikely that "honoring" our parents would add so much as a single day to the length of time most of us will spend in Yisra'el – which is the only land given to anyone by God.

The implications of this observation are further underscored by the fact it would be another forty years before just two souls in this original audience would cross the Jordan River, entering the Promised Land. By excluding most of them, while also limiting the time the few who made the crossing would spend in Yisra'el, we are compelled to consider the spiritual intent of these words because a superficial interpretation of this instruction does not lead to a rational result.

To more completely appreciate the spiritual meaning of this divine prescription for living, let's consider the graphic symbols Yahowah used to write the most telling words in this Instruction. "Father," from *'ab*, was written Aleph 𐤀 Beyth 𐤁, the initial characters in the Hebrew alphabet – and indeed the origin of the English word. When we say "alphabet," we are essentially saying "father." The

ᗒ Aleph was originally drawn in the form of a ram's head which was symbolic of "power, might, leadership, and authority" as well as "being part of the flock." A ram represented the "ability to perform, doing whatever work was required." It implies that Yahowah wants to be one with His sheep, living with them while guiding and protecting them.

In Ancient Hebrew, the ᗐ Beyth was shaped to depict the floor plan of a tent enclosure – one with a single entrance. It was symbolic of "entering a home and being protected within a shelter, being part of a family and living in a house." We may thus infer that the "ᗐᗒ – Father" being represented in this exhortation is the "Mighty One with the power and authority to build His home, doing the work required to lead His Family inside, sheltering them" so that they come to live with Him in the Promised Land.

The Hebrew word "'em – Mother" begins the same way with the Aleph ᗒ conveying all of the power, authority, and capability symbolized by a ram's head. But this time, it is combined with the Hebrew letter, Mem ᗰ, which was originally drawn to depict the "life-giving, sustaining, and cleansing properties of water." The character was drawn to depict waves upon the sea. So, we may conclude that the "ᗰᗒ – Mother" depicted in this Godly instruction, who has the "power to impart life, the ability to sustain it, and the will to do whatever is required to cleanse Her children, perfecting them," is: Our Spiritual Mother.

For those who may be thinking that I'm overreaching here by referring to the symbolism inherent in the ancient Hebrew letters Yahowah actually etched in stone, you may find it comforting to know that, of the eight Dead Sea Scroll parchments, written in Ancient and Paleo Hebrew, seven of the eight were from Towrah scrolls – which is where Yahowah's Instructions are found. And as we shall see as we dig deeper into God's revelation, almost every

Hebrew word, name, and title, including His own, are most easily and effectively understood when we consider the alphabet originally chosen to represent them.

In this light, while most people are comfortable envisioning God as our Heavenly Father, relatively few are open to the realization that the Set-Apart Spirit (errantly depicted as the "Holy Spirit" or, worse, the "Holy Ghost") is Maternal. And yet, in *Bare'syth* / Genesis 1:27, Yahowah unequivocally revealed: **"So, God created 'Adam in His image** (*tselem* – resemblance, pattern, and model). **In the image** (*tselem*) **of the Almighty, He created him. Male and female, He created them."** God, therefore, in addition to being paternal, has a maternal nature.

When we consider the ways He manifests and describes Himself, as our "*'ab* – Father" and in the form of the "*ruwach qodesh* – Set-Apart Spirit," we find that one of the titles is masculine and the other is feminine. Moreover, in keeping with the alphabetic symbols which comprise "ᴍᵥ – Mother," *ruwach*, a feminine noun, is defined as the "breath of life." It is directly associated with *ruwah* which means "to be completely covered and saturated with water." Further, while the primary meaning of *qodesh*, the adjective which describes the Spirit's nature, is "set apart," it also conveys the idea of "purifying and cleansing" someone or something so that they appear perfect in Yahowah's presence, further associating ᴍᵥ's etymology.

It is also interesting to note that Yahowah's name is feminine, as is God's "*beryth* – Covenant" and "*towrah* – Teaching." Yahuwdah is feminine as is Yisra'el. Four of the Miqra'ey are feminine as well: Matsah, Shabuw'ah, Taruw'ah, and Sukah. Pesach is masculine because the Lamb is male. And Bikuwrym is masculine because the Firstborn Child was a son. I suspect that Kipurym is also a masculine noun because it denotes the day Yahowah will return.

Two final thoughts for those who might still cling to the notion that God is telling us to honor our birth mother and father as opposed to our Spiritual Mother and Heavenly Father: First, speaking to Yisra'el through the prophet *Howsha'* / Hosea, Yahowah said: **"Rebuke (***rib* – quarrel in a state of hostility, be in opposition and contend with) **your mother, bring a lawsuit forth to prosecute her: for she is not my wife, neither am I her husband."** (*Howsha'* / He Saves / Hosea 2:2) Their mothers, like their fathers, had corrupted and ignored Yah's advice, and they had chased after false gods and goddesses, particularly "*Ba'al* – the Lord" and "*'Asherah* – the Blessed." They were leading their children astray. And in particular, their decision to worship 'Asherah as the Queen of Heaven was something God found repulsive.

Since it is relevant, if I might indulge your patience a bit longer, in the same prophetic book we referenced a moment ago, we find: **"My people (***'am***) are destroyed and they will perish (***damah* – they are cut off and will cease to exist (niphal perfect – telling us that the people have actively participated in their own absolute demise)) **because of (***min* – from) **a lack of understanding (***bely* – corrupted information, inadequate knowledge, and deficient discernment).**

Indeed, because (*ky***) you (***'atah***) have totally avoided and rejected (***ma'as* – have spurned and despised, literally refused and disdained (qal perfect – revealing that the avoidance was complete at this time and the rejection was literal)) **knowledge and understanding (***da'ath* – information and discernment), **so then (***wa***) I will consistently reject and avoid you (***ma'as* – I will actually dissociate from you and will rebuff you (qal imperfect)) **from serving as authorized officials (***kahan* – from acting as counselors, ministers, and emissaries) **on My behalf (***la* – for Me).**

Since (*wa*) **you have continually ignored** (*shakah* – you have consistently overlooked and literally forgotten, you have lost sight of the significance of and responded improperly to (qal imperfect consecutive)) **the *Towrah* | Teaching of your God** (*Towrah 'elohym* – your God's Instruction, Guidance, and Direction)**, I also** (*'any gam*) **will consistently ignore your children** (*shakah ben* – I will overlook your sons, forget about your children, and view them as worthless)**.**" (*Howsha'* / He Saves / Hosea 4:6)

Those who neglect Yahowah's Towrah Instructions are dissociated from Him. But more than this, by doing so, parents dissuade their children from developing a relationship with God.

The tendency of a child to adopt and respect their parents' religion is the cause of this predicament. **"So, as** (*ka*) **they grew and became more powerful** (*rabab* – they became more numerous and influential)**, all the more** (*ken*) **they missed the way** (*chata'* – they erred, retreated, and went in the wrong direction)**.**

They exchanged (*muwr* – substituted) **their reputation and reward** (*kabowd* – their honor and respect, their glorious manifestation of power, status, and forthcoming abundance) **for** (*ba*) **shame** (*qalown* – dishonor and disgrace, ignominy and infamy)**.** (*Howsha'* 4:7)

They feed upon (*'akal*) **the wrongdoing and misguided beliefs** (*chata'th* – the iniquity and propitiations, the errant ways and sinful offerings) **of My people** (*'am* – My family)**.**

And so (*wa*) **therefore** (*'el* – accordingly)**, their perverse distortions** (*'awon* | *'aown* – their errant perversions and corruptions, their tendency to twist and distort) **mislead and beguile** (*nasha'* – sweep away, deceive, and indebt) **their souls** (*nepesh*)**.** (*Howsha'* 4:8)

68

And so (*wa*), **it will come to be** (*hayah* – it was, is, and will be) **as with** (*ka*) **the people** (*ha 'am*), **so as with** (*ka*) **the ministers** (*kohen* – the priests who officiate)**.**

I will consider and record (*wa paqad* – I will impute and reckon) **their ways** (*derek* – their conduct and way of life) **against them** (*'al*)**. And** (*wa*) **their deeds and practices** (*ma'alal* – their actions and activities)**, I will turn upon them** (*shuwb la* – I will return to them, paying them back for what they have done)**."** (*Howsha'* / He Saves / Hosea 4:7-9)

If we were looking for additional assurance that we are not to honor the ways of our human parents but, instead, our Heavenly Father and Spiritual Mother in association with the Towrah and its Covenant, we have it now. This teaching sheds considerable light on the Second Instruction as well, affirming its spiritual perspective.

By taking our time and considering all reasonable possibilities, by evaluating each pertinent clue, we discover that highly valuing our Heavenly Father and Spiritual Mother secures the initial benefit of the Covenant: eternal life. By carefully considering what God reveals about parenting His children, by seeing God as awesome and wonderful, and by valuing God's guidance, our days can be elongated, continuing forever, enabling us to live in the Promised Land, itself serving as a metaphor for Heaven. And therein is the symbolic meaning behind this statement as well as the only rational interpretation of the Second of Seven Instructions.

ᐧ𐤔𐤉𐤅𐤔

The preceding insight into what is expected of us if we want to become a child of the Covenant explains why the Godly directive regarding our Heavenly Father and

Spiritual Mother was more vital than the next Instruction. So now in the prioritized order of things, this is what follows the Second Instruction scribed on the Second Tablet...

"You should not kill on an ongoing basis (*lo' ratsach* – you should not make a practice of taking the life of another whether by accident, revenge, manslaughter, premeditation, assassination, governmental execution, military slaughter, or murder (qal imperfect))**."** (*Shemowth* / Names / Exodus 20:13)

Just two words long, this is the Third of Seven Instructions. God does not want us to make a habit or practice of killing. And yet, by ignoring or, worse, by corrupting and twisting, Yahowah's Towrah, many commit spiritual murder, foreshortening their own lives in an act of suicide, while annihilating those of their children. God is imploring us not to do that.

We would be remiss if we didn't resolve an issue which has become the subject of many heated debates. Those who say that God asked us not to commit "murder" are correct, but so are those who insist that He instructed us not to "kill." There is no distinction in Hebrew between "killing" and "murdering," in "taking the life of another." The Hebrew word, *ratsach*, can be translated either way.

Ratsach is used in *Bamidbar* / Numbers 35:11 to address those guilty of unpremeditated and accidental killings, and thus of committing manslaughter. Then in *Bamidbar* / Numbers 35:27, *ratsach* shows someone killing as an act of revenge. In *Melekym* / 2 Kings 6:32 *ratsach* is used in association with a politically inspired assassination. The ramifications of this are significant, especially, as one considers what soldiers are asked to do in religiously and politically inspired wars.

More interesting still, *ratsach* is deployed metaphorically in *Yowb* / Job 24:14, giving additional credence to the idea that this Instruction has spiritual implications. This notion is further underscored in *Howsha'* / Hosea 6:9, where *ratsach* reveals: **"As marauding bands of robbers lie in wait for an individual, the society's religious officials and spellbinding priests kill in what amounts to premeditated spiritual murder by way of consent; for they act and engage in that which is adulterous and idolatrous, committing heinous crimes."** Yahowah defines such deadly men as despicable religious whores who are prone to incarcerate His people in the next verse.

Also relevant, this instruction was conveyed using the qal stem and imperfect conjunction. This stem not only tells us not to associate with the killing of others but, also, ties the verb's subject which is us, with the verb's action, which is refraining from killing. Then by deploying the imperfect, God is telling us that the habit or practice of killing should be avoided, thus dissociating Himself from militaries whose troops are trained to kill and from religious institutions which have robbed men of their souls for countless generations. In the imperfect then, *lo' ratsach* says that we "should not continue to foreshorten lives."

Some may be protesting at this moment saying that Yahowah asked Yahowsha' ben Nuwn to remove the hosts of religion from the land, killing them once their iniquity had become full. But even here, this was a "perfect" act, not an "imperfect" one, in that Yah's directions were limited in scope, place, purpose, and time. He has not mandated any "imperfect" ongoing and open-ended, instructions to kill.

Also, to be clear, this act was God's prerogative, not ours. He alone has that right. Life is His gift. Therefore, to create the environment where the path to eternal life could be known, Yahowah shortened the lives of those whose religion had previously disqualified them. By so doing, they would be unable to negatively influence others by discouraging them from embracing His gift.

This next Instruction, the Fourth of Seven, also encourages us to consider its deeper spiritual insights. Like the previous teaching, it was scribed in the qal stem and imperfect conjunction. Yahowah is establishing a pattern – one which reveals that our prior indiscretions, if not ongoing, no longer plague our relationship with our Heavenly Father. This explains how Dowd could slip up from time to time and still have God put it behind them and move on. It is, at least for those of us with a checkered past, a tremendous relief.

It is amazing how big a difference something as simple as a conjugation can make as we assess our standing with God. He is far from the disciplinarian that He is cast as being in Paul's letters. He isn't asking or expecting us to be perfect but, instead, knows that we are imperfect. So, He's focusing on our attitude, encouraging us to act better, to think more clearly, to respond more appropriately to get in the habit of becoming more like Him.

"You should not continue to participate in idolatrous worship or make a habit of taking another's wife (*lo' na'aph* – you should not be unfaithful by being religious and pursuing other gods nor have sexual relations with a married woman).**"** (*Shemowth* / Names / Exodus 20:14)

Throughout the Towrah, *na'aph* is used to explicitly state that men should not take another man's wife as his own. It is never used to infer that a man can only have one wife or that we shouldn't have sexual relations with those who are unmarried. There is no edict against being promiscuous either. Further, *na'aph* is not used to state that a married woman should have only one husband or to restrict affairs with unmarried men. The Towrah is silent on such issues. Therefore, the Towrah's use of *na'aph* is

72

inconsistent with the way the English word is portrayed today.

But even in the Towrah, the context conveys a much more important and deeper, indeed more relevant meaning. Consider this from *Qara'* / Leviticus 20:1-10:

"And Yahowah spoke to Moseh, saying, (*Qara'* 20:1) 'Again you shall say to the children of Yisra'el, "Whosoever of the children of Yisra'el or of the foreigners who live and travel through Yisra'el, who gives of his offspring, and thus of what he sows including his children, unto Molek (the god and king of the Ammonites and Phoenicians), shall die a second death. So, the people of the Land shall assemble to cast vocal aspersions, as if piling up stones. (*Qara'* 20:2)

I will set My presence against that individual and will cut him off, separating him, from the core of his people because he has given of his seed, and thus his children, to Molek in order to corrupt My set-apart place while also desecrating and ritually defiling, even profaning, My set-apart name. (*Qara'* 20:3)

If the people of the Land make any attempt to conceal, blinding their eyes so as to ignore the individual who has given of his seed, and thus his children, to Molek (the false god and king worshiped by the Phoenicians and Ammonites), who fail to see to it that he is dispatched and perishes, (*Qara'* 20:4) then I will be determined to establish My presence against that individual and against his family, and will cut him off and separate those who commit spiritual adultery and religious whoredom, indeed, idolatry (*zanah*), with Molek from among their people. (*Qara'* 20:5)

The soul who turns to or appears before their deceased forefathers in ancestor worship, venerating saints, or contacting familial spirits via a séance or through mediums or pursues a spiritualist who claims

to know heavenly secrets or conveys the message of these spirits, who commit spiritual adultery and religious whoredom, indeed, idolatry (*zanah*) after them, I will place My presence against that soul and will cut him off from among his people. (*Qara'* 20:6)

Dedicate yourself to being observant and then different than those who pursue these common and popular practices, thereby being set apart, for I am Yahowah, your God. (*Qara'* 20:7)

Again, you should be observant, closely examining and carefully considering the prescriptions and conditions I have inscribed and then act upon them. I, Yahowah, am set apart (and thus not found among the common, popular, or pervasive practices of man). (*Qara'* 20:8)

For everyone who slights or diminishes the importance of, or trifling with, his Father or his Mother shall surely die for the reason that he has rebuffed and insulted, maligned and denigrated, his Father and his Mother, and his lifeblood is upon him. (*Qara'* 20:9)

Furthermore, the individual who acts inappropriately by taking (*na'aph*) a man's wife, improperly desiring (*na'aph*) his neighbor's woman, the unfaithful and idolatrous (*na'aph*) man and the unfaithful and idolatrous (*na'aph*) woman shall surely die.'" (*Qara'* / Called Out / Leviticus 20:10)

Yahowah is announcing His animosity against his people's propensity to be religious and then stating the consequence of participating in these popular human endeavors. This is not a declaration against adultery, of having more than one wife or multiple girlfriends, or even of a married man or woman having an affair with someone who isn't married.

In the prophets, *na'aph* is also deployed to warn us against engaging in religious affairs with false gods. An example of this is found in *Yirma'yah* / Jeremiah 3:8-11:

"'I saw all of the many occasions where, by turning away into apostasy, through abandonment and renunciation, Yisra'el committed adultery (*na'aph*).

So, I let her loose and I sent her away, giving her a written letter of divorce, thereby cutting ties. And yet, her treacherously deceitful sister, Yahuwdah, showed no respect, and went on to also play the role of an idolatrous religious harlot (*zanah*). (*Yirma'yah* 3:8)

It came to be through the voice of her infidelity, idolatry, and whoredom (*zanuwth*) that she corrupted and profaned, polluting and defiling the Land and thereby committed adultery by engaging in idolatrous worship (*na'aph*) with stones and with wooden timbers (such as idols and crosses). (*Yirma'yah* 3:9)

And yet considering all of this, her treacherously deceitful sister, Yahuwdah, has not changed her attitude and returned to Me with all of her heart, her attitude, motivations, and judgment, but instead is a disappointing and deceptive fraud and false witness,' prophetically declares Yahowah. (*Yirma'yah* 3:10)

Then, Yahowah said unto me, 'The attempts at this time to appear righteous and justified of Yisra'el regarding her turning way into apostasy through abandonment and renunciation are more covert and dishonest, even duplicitous and disloyal, therefore, spiritually adulterous, than Yahuwdah.'" (*Yirma'yah* / Jeremiah 3:11)

Na'aph is used somewhat interchangeably with *zanah* in both of these citations, albeit we get the sense that the former speaks more about violating the "*beryth* – covenant marriage vow." And I suspect that this is what each of these instructions has sought to underscore with their focus on our Heavenly Father and Spiritual Mother and with the admonitions that we should not take the life of another or be inappropriately unfaithful.

This is, in fact, the fourth familial reference Yahowah has made. He has spoken of His concern that fathers fail to protect their children, of sons and daughters observing the *Shabat*, of children considering the full significance of our Heavenly Father and Spiritual Mother so that we might live forever in the place He has provided for us and, now, of being inappropriately unfaithful. These references underscore our Heavenly Father's affinity for His *Beryth* | Covenant – a word which is based upon *beyth*, meaning "family, home, and household." Yahowah's *Beryth* | Covenant is accurately defined as a "family-oriented relationship based upon a marriage vow and protective home environment where God's children thrive."

God's lone objective in creating the universe was to enjoy a loving family. As proof, when the existing universe is replaced, only the children of His Covenant will remain.

The reason this Instruction is important is because, by acting unfaithfully and inappropriately, we shatter symbols dear to Yahowah's heart: husbands and wives becoming fathers and mothers in relationships akin to marriage to conceive loving families, providing for their children in protective homes, nourishing them.

Once again, by using the qal stem and imperfect conjunction, God is not only telling us not to make a practice of acting in a manner which is destructive of our relationship with Him and especially by being religious, but, also, is encouraging us to refrain from continually doing something which would cause others to be derelict in their relationship with Yah. To this end, the imperfect also adds an enduring perspective. There is an ongoing consequence of religious whoredom that Yahowah wants us to avoid because it is lethal to building the loving family He envisions. So, in the imperfect, *lo' na'ap* says that we "should not continue to be religiously unfaithful or inappropriate in our relationships."

God did not tell men and women that they could not have sex with multiple partners, He did not tell us that we ought not have more than one spouse. He did not even tell us that we shouldn't have an affair with an unmarried man or woman. He neither encouraged nor discouraged such things. This Instruction was not about promiscuity, monogamy, or sexuality. It is about not cheating ourselves by worshiping other gods. And while that may sound strange to modern ears, keep in mind that for most of man's history, religion was a highly erotic experience, replete with temple prostitutes. Women seduced men into worshiping their gods.

Furthermore, it was religious impropriety, not homosexuality, which was addressed here. And while that must be a shock to conservative Christians who relish condemning homosexuals in the name of their god, what I am about to say will likely send them away kicking and screaming. Yahowah had little if anything to say about homosexuality. There is not even a word for "homosexual" in the Hebrew lexicon.

There are only two statements in the whole of the Towrah that address the issue of men being with other men, or at least with boys. And while neither speaks of sex, the intended meaning behind both requires a bit of investigative etymology because they are challenging to translate.

At issue are the following words: 1) Why was *'ysh* used initially to speak of "an individual male" rather than "*'adam* – man?" 2) Why was *shakab* used to speak of "lying down in a horizontal position for rest or sleep, for sex or lodging, for meditation or contemplation, for

77

jubilation or sorrow, or in sickness and death" rather than "*bow'* – come into?" 3) Should *'eth* be translated as "with" or "against?" 4) Why was *zakar* chosen as the object of these statements when its primary meaning is "to remember?" While its secondary connotation refers to "an adolescent or young boy," even to "a religious prostitute," there are far more common words for man, such as *'adam*, *'ysh*, or *'enosh*. 5) How does one define *mishakab*, the compound of *my* and *shakab*, such that it is accurate and actionable in these sentences? 6) Which of the many connotations of *'ishah* are we to use, "woman, wife, fire, female, mother, or burnt offering?" and 7) What is the proper way to deal with the repetition of "*muwth* – death," and how do we apply the highly unusual hofal stem which conveys a double negation of freewill?

Especially interesting with regard to translating *mishakab* in *Qara'* / Leviticus 18:22 and 20:13, is how it is used the first time it appears in the Towrah. In *Bare'syth* / Genesis 49:4, Ya'aqob is on his deathbed while giving final blessings to each of his children. But rather than commend Reuben, Ya'aqob condemns him because of what he had done to humiliate his father in an act of revenge for the sake of his mother.

Since Ya'aqob's assessment of Reuben's grievance against him is the most irrefutable and rational way to appreciate why *mishakab* was used by Yahowah in both of the supposed condemnations of homosexuality, let's see why Ya'aqob conveyed his frustration with *mishakab*.

Ya'aqob's second wife, Rachel, who was Leah's younger sister, died giving birth to *ben 'Ony* (son of wicked idolatry, iniquity, and sorrow) whom Ya'aqob renamed *Benyamyn* | Benjamin. But rather than turn to and comfort Leah, his first wife, and Rachel's older sister, moving her into his tent at this time, Ya'aqob elevated the status of his concubine, Bilhah, who had been Rachel's handmaid. For slighting his mother in this way, Reuben may have sought to embarrass his father.

Therefore, it was an act of revenge and degradation...

"And it came to pass (*wa hayah*) **while Yisra'el lived** (*ba shakan Yisra'el* – with Ya'aqob now dwelling) **in that Land** (*ba ha 'erets ha hy'*)**, that** (*wa*) **Reuben** (*Ra'uwben* – Witness the Son, Leah's firstborn with Ya'aqob) **went** (*halak* – traveled by walking (qal imperfect consecutive)) **and** (*wa*) **laid** (*shakab* – was in a horizontal position for rest or sleep, for sex or lodging, for meditation or contemplation, for jubilation or sorrow, or in sickness and death (qal imperfect)) **with and against** (*'eth*) **Bilhah** (*Bilhah* – Troublesome, Terrorizing, and Dreadfully Destructive, Rachel's handmaid whom she offered to Ya'aqob as a concubine and mother of Dan and Naphtali)**, his father's concubine** (*pilegesh 'ab huw' huw'* – his father's paramour or illicit lover of low status dedicated to pleasing her owner in a polygamous relationship)**. And Yisra'el heard of it** (*wa Yisra'el shama' hy'*)**."** (*Bare'syth* / Genesis 35:22)

The vivid memory of that intentionally degrading and humiliating act still in his mind, haunting him, Ya'aqob said the following to his son, Reuben, while dying...

"Impulsive and reckless (*pachaz* – turbulent, insolent, arrogant, wanton, uncontrolled and self-willed with a false sense of confidence and importance, failing to appreciate or contemplate the overall significance or ramifications of one's actions) **as the sea** (*ka ha maym* – as floodwaters or a river of tears)**, you will not prevail** (*'al yatar* – you will not persevere, excel, or prosper, nor will you be among the remnant who are abundantly enriched (hifil imperfect jussive))**.

Because, indeed** (*ky* – for the express and emphasized reason)**, you lifted yourself up** (*'alah* – you genuinely got carried away in the moment and you ascended (qal perfect)) **to call your father's bed into question** (*mishakab 'ab 'atah* – questioning the who and why of lying down for rest, sleep, or sex, even for meditation or contemplation, for jubilation or sorrow, or in sickness and death; from a compound of *my* – to question and *shakab* – to become horizontal**).**

Therefore, at that time (*'az* – simultaneously then as a result**), you defiled and dishonored** (*chalal* – you violated and treated with contempt, diminishing the status of and profaning so as to humiliate) **my bed** (*yatsuwa' 'any* – where I had laid down and slept) **in an attempt to rise above** (*'alah* – so as to elevate oneself (qal perfect))**."** (*Bare'syth* / Genesis 49:4)

Considering the purpose of the Covenant, which is to produce children for God's Family, and Ya'aqob's role in it as the father of Yisra'el, Reuben chose the wrong way to support his mother and denigrate his father. We will want to keep this in mind as we strive to accurately translate the next two statements.

Furthermore, since there is a perfectly good Hebrew word for bed, *yatsuwa'*, "*mishakab* – to question the reasons for lying down" was introduced here for a reason – and that would be to enable us to properly understand its subsequent use in the Towrah. When this same compound word is deployed in *Qara'* / Leviticus 18:22 and 20:13, we are now aware that it ought not be thoughtlessly rendered as "bed."

Moreover, we know that the term carries with it the idea of "embarrassing and humiliating someone in an act of revenge, of denigrating and dishonoring them." It is, therefore, about "imposing oneself on another in a disingenuous and shameful manner so as to put them down and debase them as victors have done to those they have vanquished." Further, those who seek to elevate their status in this way are reckless and impulsive with a false sense of self-worth. In the end they will not prevail as a consequence of perpetrating such despicable acts.

This then brings us to the first supposed declaration "against 'homosexuality.'" It reads:

"**So** (*wa* – and then)**, with or against** (*'eth* – in opposition to, with antagonism toward, accompanied by, or as an accusative sign, even plowing into) **an adolescent young boy** (*zakar* – a younger person, a male child, by way of a memorable proclamation, so that it will be recalled and remembered)**, do not lie down** (*lo' shakab* – do not constantly position oneself for rest or sleep, for sex or lodging, for meditation or contemplation, for jubilation or sorrow, nor in sickness and death (qal imperfect)) **to call the reasons for lying down into question** (*mishakab* – questioning the who, what, why, and how of lying down for rest or sleep, for sex or lodging, for meditation or contemplation, for jubilation or sorrow, or for sickness and death on a bed for reclining or bier for a corpse; from a compound of *my* – to question and *shakab* – to become horizontal) **associated with a female or with a fire** (*'ishah* – with a wife, mother, or woman, even with that which burns and is combustible, a feminine individual, or spouse, flames or burnt offering)**.**

It's (*hy'* – she's) **a detestable thing** (*towe'bah* – an abhorrent and repulsive, confusing and confounding religious practice and a detestable act of idolatrous worship which is to be rejected)**.**" (*Qara'* / Leviticus 18:22)

The second reads:

"**Also** (*wa*)**, an individual** (*'ysh* – a person (masculine)) **who** (*'asher*) **continues to lie down** (*shakab* – constantly is in a horizontal position for rest or sleep, for sex or lodging, for meditation or contemplation, for jubilation or sorrow, reclining in sickness or death (qal imperfect)) **with or against** (*'eth* – in opposition to, with antagonism toward, accompanied by, or as an accusative sign, even plowing into) **an adolescent** (*zakar* – a young boy, one's male offspring, in an especially memorable and illicit encounter with a religious prostitute, such that it deals with one's honor, cannot be forgotten, and is etched into one's memory) **to question sleeping in the bed or bier** (*mishakab* – to ponder the who, what, how, and why of lying down for rest or sleep, for sex or lodging, for meditation or contemplation, for jubilation or sorrow, or in sickness or death) **of a woman, of a wife, or of fire** (*'ishah* – of an individual female, of maternal flames, or as Gefilte fish flambé) **has performed** (*'asah* – has engaged in and done at that moment in time (qal perfect)) **an abhorrent thing** (*towe'bah* – a repulsive and confounding religious practice and a detestable act of idolatrous worship which is to be rejected).

The two of them (*shanaym hem* – both of them) **die twice over with one being forced under the control of the other** (*muwth muwth* – shall certainly perish with ongoing implications (qal infinitive hofal imperfect – a particularly descriptive verbal noun whereby the subject is compelled to force the object)). **Their lifeblood** (*dam hem*) **is upon them** (*ba hem*)." (*Qara'* / Leviticus 20:13)

With all due consideration toward how Yahowah unabashedly and painstakingly defined *mishakab* in relation to Reuben seeking to inappropriately denigrate his father, Ya'aqob, for slighting his mother, this becomes an admonition against degrading and humiliating young men and boys, especially in a familial or religious context. It is not about homosexuality. So, while it has taken some effort, clearing the air on this subject was long overdue.

That is not to say that God is supportive of homosexual behavior; I do not suspect He is, but it is to say that religious infidelity is of far greater concern to Him. Christians, encapsulated in Pauline Doctrine, and susceptible to errant translations, are prone to view homosexuality more harshly than adultery and, therefore, lash out at homosexuals while ignoring their own behavior. In so doing, they miss the message God was conveying.

Fact is, when an older man uses his power or influence to lie with an adolescent boy, the child is traumatized and degraded, causing them to question the purpose of being in bed with a woman – indeed to question the purpose of women, the role of men, and the nature of a loving relationship. A staggering percentage of bisexuals were sexually abused as children. Homosexuals and bisexuals are less likely to be caring adults. More shocking still, 45% of bisexual women have considered or attempted suicide (7 times higher than heterosexual women) followed closely by 35% of bisexual men, 30% of lesbian women, and one in every four gay men. (Bi Health Summit's 2009 Report) Further, according to an Australian study, middle-aged bi women are 24 times more likely than straight women to engage in self-harm, such as routinely cutting themselves as a coping mechanism.

This is a shrill warning to the Roman Catholic clergy, to priests who have molested millions of young men and boys. It is a harsh warning to Muslims, who love "*Bacha Bazi* – Boy Play*," chaining naked children to beds so that they can be gang-raped for weeks on end. And rabbis aren't immune either, although they attempt to silence those they have abused by running their cases through their religious courts.

It is a little-known fact, but as was the case with Reuben and Bilhah, rape isn't typically about sex, but instead about conquest and abuse, power and control. Especially in ancient times, victorious soldiers were prone to rape those they vanquished to further humiliate them.

The next Instruction on the Second Tablet is simple. And like the previous two admonitions, it is presented in the qal imperfect.

"You should not make a habit of stealing (*lo' ganab* – you should not routinely take something from others without their permission, neither kidnap nor commit robbery using deception or acting secretly)**."** (*Shemowth* / Names / Exodus 20:15)

Ganab speaks of taking something which does not belong to us by stealth, not force – always without consent and often without the victim's knowledge. It smacks of "deceit," of "outwitting" someone, and "cheating" them out of something valuable – and then of "carrying it away." All of man's religions do this very thing.

In order to once again demonstrate the religious and spiritual implications of these Divine Instructions, let's turn to *Yahowsha'* / Joshua 7:11 to see how *ganab* is used in conjunction with these ideas...

"Yisra'el (*Yisra'el* – Individuals who Strive and Struggle with God) **has erred, missing the way for the moment** (*chata'* – is wrong, having gone astray in the period of time (qal perfect))**, and also** (*gam* – moreover) **they have forgotten and repealed at this time** (*'abar* – intoxicated for the moment, they have transgressed so as to get rid of (qal perfect)) **accordingly** (*'eth*) **My Covenant** (*beryth 'any* – My family-oriented relationship agreement, My pledge and wedding vow, My contract and compact, My treaty and alliance)**, which to show the correct path to walk to benefit from the joyous relationship** (*'asher* – which to reveal the proper and narrow, straightforward and beneficial steps to get the most out of life) **I provided instruction for them** (*tsawah 'eth hem* – I offered to them to provide direction (piel perfect – at the time, the subject, God, taught the object, Yisra'el)).

And likewise (*wa gam* – moreover and furthermore)**, they have taken** (*laqach* – they have for some time grasped hold of and obtained (qal perfect)) **from** (*min*) **that which is dedicated and devoted to God's purpose and is**

prohibited because it can utterly and completely destroy (*cherem* – that which is for God's use such that it will sever the relationship and exterminate the usurper when men assert their control over His things), and thereby (*wa gam*) they have misappropriated and stolen these things without permission (*ganab* – they have taken this without the Owner's consent, committing robbery while acting secretly (qal perfect)) and also (*wa gam* – in addition to) lying to everyone, feigning submission while being deceptive and duplicitous regarding their delusions (*kachash* – failing and being disowned by disavowing the truth and improperly dealing with reality (piel perfect)), beyond which (*wa gam* – and as if that were not enough) they have placed them (*sym* – they have set them, appointing and listing them (qal perfect)) among their own belongings (*ba kaly hem* – with their implements and possessions, their equipment and tools, their weapons and possessions, even their adornments and accoutrements)." (*Yahowsha'* / Yahowah Delivers, Liberates, and Saves / Joshua 7:11)

Of all mankind's bad ideas, few things have been worse than attempting to misappropriate God's authority, testimony, and responsibility. The message of the rabbis in the Talmud is inferior to God's in the Towrah. No matter how shrill their voice, the Roman Catholic Church does not hold the keys to heaven nor influence anyone's salvation. Those who have accepted the myths of a "New Testament," a "Renewed Covenant," the "Gospel of Grace," "Salvation through Faith," a Talmud comprised of Oral Laws, a Book of Mormon, or a Quran, have missed the way.

The Covenant is Yahowah's Family. It is subject to His conditions, not man's. To suggest otherwise is to claim God's authority is a gross "*ganab* – misappropriation without the Owner's consent." All claims to the contrary are delusional.

Chaff and stubble are the antithesis of purified grain (a metaphor for saved souls). And as such, chaff represents those whose wasted lives are snuffed out for having been deceived by religious rhetoric. The spiritual message behind the Fifth of Yahowah's Seven Instructions serves to reinforce God's overt condemnation of deception. We are not to steal souls away from Yah.

As we have come to appreciate, it is also true with the negation of "*ganab* – stealing," the qal stem serves to admonish us that we should interpret this Instruction literally. And that means that we should dissociate ourselves from any religious, political, military, or economic institution which takes something away from people without their permission. To this, the imperfect conjugation reveals that there are ongoing and unfolding consequences of military, political, economic, and taxation schemes which redistribute wealth as the politically empowered see fit. Thus, by writing this in the imperfect, *lo' ganab* conveys that we "should not make a practice of taking what does not belong to us."

The Sixth of Seven Divine Instructions on the Second Tablet continues along the same theme. As has been the case with the prior three, this Instruction was not written in the imperative but was scribed in the qal imperfect.

"You should not continuously answer and respond (*lo' 'anah* – you should refrain from replying by providing testimony or consistently making a declaration) **against** (*ba*) **your neighbor's evil thoughts** (*rea' 'atah* – the sinful and improper, regretful and debilitating way of your countrymen, friends, companions, or associates) **as a deceptive or misleading** (*seqer* – false, conniving, clever, mistaken, vain, or unreliable, lying or fraudulent, useless or irrelevant) **witness** (*'ed* – source of evidence by way of testimony)." (*Shemowth* / Names / Exodus 20:16)

The essence of religion and politics is "false testimony." Nothing is more damaging, destructive, deadly, or damning. It is how Satan beguiled Chawah in the Garden of 'Eden. He misquoted God. It is how Rabbi Akiba, the fake-apostle Paul, and the false-prophet Muhammad deceived billions of gullible souls throughout the centuries. They were all liars – the very worst of the breed because they attributed their misleading testimony to God.

While we are all called to be "'ed – witnesses," our message should convey Yahowah's "'ed – testimony." That way, we will contribute the utmost good with the least possible downside risk. The bottom line is that if we are going to speak for God, we should quote Him accurately. Those who choose to serve as witnesses, must recite His testimony clearly and correctly. Do not change it, subtract from it, or add to it.

And yet, in defiance of the qal stem and imperfect conjugation in conjunction with lo' 'anah, all manner of clerics have made a practice of providing misleading and deceptive rhetoric. It isn't that everything pastors, priests, rabbis, and imams have claimed through the ages is false, but that so many lies have been woven into their statements that what has emerged from their mouths has consistently been more poisonous than nurturing.

In the end, all we really have from God is life, freewill, a conscience, and His testimony. If we corrupt it, the first three gifts are for naught.

I recognize that this Instruction is usually rendered: "You shall not bear false testimony against your neighbor." But the problem with that approach is that the primary meaning of 'anah is "to answer and respond" rather than to "testify." And since 'ed actually means "testimony," we cannot ignore 'anah.

So, rather than this Instruction serving as an admonition not to lie about one's neighbor, it was scribed to suggest that we should not deceive our neighbors by inaccurately conveying Yahowah's testimony to them. The former is a good idea, but the latter is life and death.

Those who have read the *Miqra'ey* | Invitations volume of *Yada Yahowah* are familiar with *'anah* – the operative verb in this Instruction. It has become our constant companion throughout our journey to meet and embrace Yah. We first encountered *'anah* in *Qara'* / Called Out / Leviticus 23:26-27: **"Then, Yahowah declared the Word to Moseh, saying, 'On the tenth of the seventh month is the Day of Reconciliations. This exists as a set-apart and called-out Invitation to Meet with you. And your soul should respond and answer (*'anah* – should reply, making a declaration after engaging in thought, vocally communicating while), appearing before and approaching the feminine aspect of the light so as to approach Yahowah.'"**

And yet, even when confronted with Yahowah etching this explicit Instruction in stone, asking us not to respond by testifying falsely, Jewish and Christian clerics have rendered *'anah* as "afflict," in correlation with *Yowm Kipurym*. By doing so, they have falsely promoted the religious notion that the means to reconcile our relationship with God is to injure and deprive ourselves. As a result of their misleading witness, as few as one soul in a million properly responds to Yahowah's Invitation to be Called Out and Meet with Him.

Lastly, *ra'a*, which is almost always rendered as "neighbor," is part of a family of highly derogatory terms, including *ra'*, *ra'a*, and *ra'ah*. Collectively, they are the harbingers of evil, speaking of the incorrect and improper, regretful and debilitating, sinful and wicked ways of our countrymen, friends, companions, associates, and neighbors. So then when translated accurately and completely, we have a much better idea of the nature of the response Yah is encouraging us to avoid.

When we are confronted by political diatribes, religious rhetoric, cultural mores, and conspiratorial myths, we are being called to respond truthfully, providing answers which correct the misguided notions of those around us. We are being called to be lights in a dark world, to be beacons of truth in a sea of deceit.

Yahowah wants us to be like Dowd. He is calling us to unabashedly expose and condemn man's errant suppositions, no matter how popular, deeply seated, or revered. Then, and only then, will our testimony be consistent with His, as God routinely condemns before He commends.

Our Heavenly Father concluded His written testimony on the Second Tablet by encouraging us not to covet that which belongs to others. Sadly, however, man's governance remains rooted in this very thing. Rabbis craved the authority which was rightly God's and thereby empowered and enriched themselves. Paul, a wannabe rabbi by training, alleged God's authority to claim the Gentiles as his own. The Roman Catholic Church sought the allegiance of pagans, and so it stole their religion and claimed it as their own. Muhammad was a thief. His religion was little more than a means to satiate his lust for power, sex, and money. Rabbis are the gold standard when it comes to embezzling the religious.

Communism exists because the poor covet their neighbor's prosperity. And in our Western democracies, voters have consistently displayed their desires, choosing tax and spend policies which redistribute wealth from those who earn it to those who crave it. The popularity of the Socialist political candidate, Bernie Sanders, especially among younger Americans, serves as proof that the nation has become the antithesis of what Yahowah is encouraging…

"'You should not make a practice out of desiring (*lo' chamad* – you should not habitually covet, delighting in, lusting for, craving, nor seek pleasure from (qal imperfect)) **your neighbor's** (*rea' 'atah* – your countryman's, friend's, companion's, or associate's inappropriate behavior and improper opinions, nor the sadness seen in their) **home or household** (*beyth* – family or house).

You should not continuously covet (*lo' chamad* – you should not desire, lust for, crave, nor seek pleasure from on an ongoing basis (qal imperfect)) **your improper neighbor's** (*rea' 'atah* – your countryman's, friend's, companion's, or associate's inappropriate behavior with, their misguided opinions regarding, or the sadness seen in their) **wife or woman** (*'ishah* – of an individual female, of maternal flames, or as Gefilte fish flambé)**, or** (*wa*) **his male or female servants** (*'ebed huw' wa 'amah huw'* – his employees or officials, the working men and women serving him)**, his comings and goings or his domesticated animals** (*sowr huw' wa chamowr huw'* – that which is capable of providing mobility and bearing a load, carrying cargo, his material assets, his belongings and possessions, means of transport, food, and production, namely his cattle or donkeys)**, or anything** (*wa kol*) **which is associated** (*'asher*) **with** (*la* – regarding) **your maligned neighbor's errant opinions or inappropriate behavior** (*rea' 'atah* – your countryman's, friend's, companion's, or associate's disconcerting thoughts, evil principles, or shameful ways).'"** (*Shemowth* / Names / Exodus 20:17)

The violation of this, Yahowah's Seventh Instruction, is the root of all evil. Desiring that which does not belong to them has motivated clerics, kings, merchants, and generals throughout the ages. They have conquered, plundered, and subjugated the masses, stealing their wives, enslaving their children, robbing their land, and confiscating their possessions.

Here the qal stem serves to discourage us from associating with the covetous schemes of religious, political, military, or economic institutions. And the imperfect affirms that there are ongoing and unfolding consequences of habitually desiring that which belongs to others. So, by scribing this in the imperfect, *lo' chamad* reveals that we "should not make a practice of coveting." When people continually desire what others own or enjoy, they become less than what they might otherwise have been. Redistributing wealth is counterproductive, economically stifling and character-destroying.

Moreover, neither our neighbor, countryman, friend, companion, nor associate owns anything of enduring value. Why covet power when the Covenant empowers? Why covet wealth when the Covenant enriches? Why covet a neighbor's wife and children when Yahowah's Covenant incorporates us into God's Family?

Speaking of family, this Instruction keeps our focus on the Covenant with references to "*beyth* – home" and "*'ishah* – wife." And it, like so many of the others, was scribed using the imperfect conjugation. This reveals that our Heavenly Father wants what is best for His children, but He is not waiting for us to make a mistake so that He can pounce on us declaring us "guilty." He expects very little from us and encourages us to refrain from doing things which are harmful to ourselves and hurtful to others. He is in the business of perfecting the imperfect. That is the Towrah's purpose.

In the imperfect, we also see how it was possible for a flawed individual like *Dowd* | David to be so beloved by God. As a child of the Covenant, Yahowah embraced the good in him and simply moved past his foibles as the man, himself, grew beyond them. And just like Dowd, in the

91

imperfect, we too can live, grow, and even flourish within this standard.

☥Υ☥ᴶ

3

Choq | Prescriptions

Speaking with You…

Moseh reiterated the message Yahowah had spoken to the Children of Yisra'el at the base of Mount Choreb. The more they heard it, the more of it they would retain and understand.

Much of which God had etched upon the stone Tablets, the great liberator and prophet reiterated, revealing how these principles for living would lead to a long and fulfilling life. And because he wrote down every word of what he and Yahowah had said, memorializing them in writing for all time, it is as if we were there.

As we ponder the implications of Moseh's introduction to, and Yahowah's commentary on, the Ten Statements – Part Two – remember where we are in place and time. Yahowah, working with the man of His choosing, an old codger no one else would have chosen, had just freed His people from the worst forms of human oppression: religious, political, military, and economic. This man was not a great orator. He was not a paradigm of virtue. He was not tolerant or accepting, soft-spoken or accommodating. He was not even willing – not initially.

Nonetheless, Moseh had some unique and enormously important qualifications for this job. He was the only person who not only knew the mindset of Mitsraym's leadership, their beliefs and vulnerabilities, their religious and political doctrines, social and economic edicts, military and patriotic propensities, but had also walked away from them.

Therefore, God did not need to waste His time, or, more importantly, suffer the irritation of teaching Moseh the many reasons He despised such things. And Moseh was both direct and brilliant, never mincing words and never bereft of understanding. He was a quick study, always able to make the kind of connections which lead to understanding. And he was both an inquiring student and an effective teacher. He was also a shepherd.

These insights are important because we tend to project characteristics upon historical personages such that the resulting caricature suits our ideals, not God's. Such is the case with casting Charlton Heston in the role of Moses. It is why the Christian "Jesus" bears no resemblance to Dowd. In most people's perceptions, Dowd is the uncircumcised and feminized porcelain white Romanesque figure Michelangelo carved for the amusement of his Church, not the passionate and intellectual lyricist with flaming red hair and gruff personality who wrote the Psalms or the resolute warrior who defended his people.

It is vastly superior for us to not only deal with reality, and go where the words lead, but to seek to appreciate why Yahowah chose the men and women He did. What is it about each one of them that made these guys the right choice for each particular mission, from safe passage to relationship, from liberation to lyrics, and from prophetic pronouncements to future fulfillments? When we come to appreciate such things, we can not only better understand the nature of the relationship Yahowah is desirous of achieving with us, but we can also seek to develop some of the same attributes that attracted God to these men. We can even come to better appreciate who He has chosen to work with to lead His people out of harm's way in the troubled days which lie before us.

Also relevant to this moment in time and to the one we are approaching, there is a reason that God began His soliloquy by drawing our attention to what He had just accomplished – liberating His family from the crucibles of human oppression – and why He would return to this subject in connection with this presentation on the purpose of the Shabat. The world has now come full circle and as we approach the thousand-year celebration of the Shabat of Sukah, with the Time of Ya'aqob's Troubles menacingly lurking on our horizon, it is time for another exodus. Are you ready?

Yahowah has arranged for His favorite liberator and shepherd, the most articulate and brilliant man who has ever lived, His beloved Son and anointed Messiah, the King of Yisra'el, to accompany Him upon His impending return and then guide His people thereafter. And to the surprise of many, that man's name is *Dowd* | David, not "Jesus." But in the meantime, there is much work to be done. So, we are going to do more than just translate and contemplate the reprisal of the Ten Statements as God's words are found here in *Dabarym* / Deuteronomy 5, we are going to expose the rationale behind them…

"Moseh (*wa Moseh* – the One who Draws Out) **invited** (*qara' 'el* – summoned and welcomed, meeting with and calling out to for the purpose of reading and reciting to (qal imperfect – establishing a genuine relationship with ongoing implications)) **all of** (*kol*) **Yisra'el** (*Yisra'el* – Individuals who Engage and Endure with God)**, and he said to them** (*wa 'amar 'el hem* – he spoke on behalf of God to them)**, 'Choose to listen** (*shama'* – opt to hear) **this day** (*ha yowm* – at this time [from 4QDeut])**, Yisra'el** (*Yisra'el*)**, to the clearly communicated prescriptions which have been engraved** (*'eth ha choq* – to the thoughts which are inscribed offering an allotment and share, to that which is carved in stone to cut us into the relationship) **along with the means to exercise good judgment and resolve disputes** (*wa ha mishpat* – as well as to the way to question the who, what, where, why, and how of justice and being judicial so as to be vindicated; from *ma* – to question and *shaphat* – to judge and decide), **which, to show the correct and beneficial way** (*'asher* – which to reveal the correct path to walk to get the most out of life and this relationship), **I am communicating** (*'any dabar* – I am conveying using written and spoken words (qal participle)) **in your hearing** (*ba 'ozen 'atah* – for your ears) **this day** (*ha yowm*).

You should choose of your own volition to learn about them (*wa lamed 'eth hem* – you should want to gather in this information and respond appropriately, instructing others what you have been taught regarding them (qal perfect consecutive)), **closely examining and carefully considering them** (*wa shamar la hem* – observing them under the auspices of freewill, becoming aware of, contemplating, and then celebrating them (qal perfect consecutive)) **so as to act upon them** (*la 'asah hem* – such that you engage and approach with them (qal infinitive construct)).'" (*Dabarym* / Words / Deuteronomy 5:1)

If only Yahuwdah and Yisra'el had done and now would do as Moseh encouraged: listen and learn, observe and act. What a wonderful world it would be!

Focus upon what matters most: Yahowah's clearly communicated prescriptions for living and God's means to exercise good judgment and resolve disputes. Listen and learn, observe and act, and everything else will fall into place.

If I could work miracles, I'd stop every reader right here, and ask them to read, and then reread *Dabarym* 5:1 seven times, maybe even seven times seven, each time pausing to reflect on the merit of this approach when it comes to the Word of God: read and recite, listen and learn, closely examine and carefully consider, and then act and engage.

Way back 3,448 years ago, Moseh did as I am striving to do for you, which is to provide commentary along with an amplified presentation of the Word of God – this because Yahowah's introduction to the Ten Statements was considerably briefer: **"Then** (*wa*)**, God** (*'elohym*) **conveyed** (*dabar*) **all of** (*kol*) **these statements using words** (*ha dabarym*)**, in our presence** (*'eth*)**, providing perspective** (*ha 'eleh*)**, by saying** (*'amar*)**:..."** (*Shemowth* / Exodus 20:1)

Moseh's presentation was enriched by including *choq* | inscribed prescriptions for living and *mishpat* | the means to execute good judgment. In his introduction, he encouraged us to *lamed* | learn by being *shamar* | observant. By doing so, we are prepared to *'asah* | engage in the relationship Yahowah intended by *'asah* | acting upon these Instructions.

The greatest of the prophets and cherished liberator realized something exceptionally profound...

"Yahowah (*Yahowah* – as directed in His *towrah* – teaching regarding His *hayah* – existence)**, our God** (*'elohym 'anachnuw*)**, has cut** (*karat* – has made and established, creating through separating, operating using a sharp blade (qal perfect)) **a Covenant** (*beryth* – a family-oriented relationship, a mutually beneficial and binding contract) **with us** (*'im 'anachnuw*) **in Choreb** (*ba Choreb* – in the desolation of the desert along a knife-shaped section of stone [where the Towrah was revealed])**."** (*Dabarym* 5:2)

Yahowah, His *Towrah* | Teaching and His *Beryth* | Covenant are inseparable, as God leads us through His words to His Family. And while there is but one God, one Towrah, and one Covenant, Yahowah's Teaching and His Family have evolved to suit the needs of His Children. Our Heavenly Father's instructions to, and His relationships with, 'Adam and Chawah, Noach and his family,

'Abraham and Sarah, Yitschaq and Ya'aqob were conveyed and developed orally as He met with and spoke to these seven individuals. But over the centuries, Yisra'el grew, with over a million souls gathered before God at this time.

That is far too many for consistent and effective personalized one-on-one guidance, especially with mankind's propensity to interpret conversations differently, which would lead to unnecessary contention. Therefore, God appropriately memorialized His *Towrah* | Teaching, confirming it in writing, and therein He reaffirmed His Covenant by sharing how it had developed.

It took me a decade or more to come to this same realization – that the Ten Statements are instrumental to the Covenant. Yahowah, in sharing them, reinforced the instructive conditions of the Beryth.

Since Yahowah communicated one-on-one with Yisra'el's forefathers, and did so verbally, this was a remarkably different experience.

"Yahowah (*Yahowah* – written as directed by His *towrah* – teaching) **cut** (*karat* – made and established through separation (qal perfect)) **this Covenant** (*'eth ha beryth ha zo'th* – this specific relationship agreement, particular family-oriented compact, mutually beneficial and binding contract, and marriage vow) **for us** (*'eth 'anachnuw* – surely because**), not with our fathers** (*lo' 'eth 'aby 'anachnuw* – before this time, it could not have been this way in the company of our forefathers**), but for those of us here today** (*'anachnuw' 'el leh poh yowm* – for those of us in this place at this time) – **indeed for all of us who are alive at this time** (*ky kol 'anachnuw chay* – for all of those living among us [from 4QDeut])**."** (*Dabarym* 5:3)

This would not be the last time Yahowah's Towrah and Covenant would grow and evolve. God's relationships

98

with 'Adam and Noach foreshadowed the Covenant which was later established with 'Abraham and Sarah. It was passed on through Yitschaq and Ya'aqob. And now His Guidance has been codified in the Towrah, with Moseh having done so before the Children of Yisra'el on this day.

Nothing has changed since that time. However, in Year 6000 Yah, God has promised to renew His *Beryth* | Covenant by writing His *towrah* | guidance inside of us so that, as a spiritual family, we are equipped to grow and prosper through dimensions and time. As such, over the long march of history, the Towrah and Covenant have been and shall be expressed in three different, yet consistent, ways.

This must have been an extraordinary experience...

"Appearing before us and in our very presence, face to face (*paneh ba paneh* – His personal existence and identity turned and directed toward us)**, Yahowah** (𐤉𐤄𐤅𐤄 – a transliteration of *YaHoWaH* as instructed in His *towrah* – teaching regarding His *hayah* – existence) **spoke** (*dabar* – communicated using words, conversing (piel perfect)) **with you** (*'im 'atem* – in your company, engaged in a relationship with you) **at the mountain** (*ba ha har* – within the ridgeline) **out of the midst** (*min tawek* – from the center and through the middle) **of the fire** (*ha 'esh* – of the flames)**."** (*Dabarym* 5:4)

Moseh is setting the scene, bringing us into the picture, and sharing this magnificent moment with us. It is almost as if we can feel the warmth of God's fiery light caressing our faces.

There is part of me that would have loved to have been a witness, to see Yah's light, to hear God's voice, to experience His presence. And yet, because of what He provided this day, we are far better equipped to know God than any of those who experienced this magnificent spectacle, save Moseh. We can do as we are doing, closely examining and carefully considering every word God and His prophet memorialized on our behalf, examining each nuance as if assessing the prismatic facets of the Hope Diamond.

"**And** (*wa* – but as for [from 4QDeut]) **I was present, standing** (*'anoky 'amad* – I stood, present and accounted for, appointed and sustained, enduring (qal participle)), **discerning insights while making the connections necessary to better appreciate** (*bayn* – receiving the revelation while discerning its meaning so as to respond properly to, or in between) **Yahowah** (*Yahowah* – God's name transliterated as guided by His *towrah* – instructions on His *hayah* – existence) **for you, such that you would understand** (*wa bayn 'atem* – and also so that you would more fully comprehend by making the appropriate connections, thereby replying appropriately to) **Him in this moment and throughout time** (*ba ha 'eth ha huw'* – Him now and after the passing of time, even in the right moment in time) **by conspicuously providing this information to you in a straightforward manner, declaring and expounding upon** (*la nagad la 'atah* – announcing and making publicly known right in front of you, reporting in plain sight to you (hifil infinitive construct)) **the words** (*ha dabarym* – the statements and accounts [plural in 1QDeut]) **of Yahowah** (𐤉𐤄𐤅𐤄 – the pronunciation of *YaHoWaH*), **your God** (*'elohym 'atah* – our Almighty [from 1QDeut])**.**" (*Dabarym* 5:5)

This, too, is argumentative and enlightening. Moseh is revealing that the Towrah and these Words inspire *bayn* | insights which lead to understanding. By *bayn* | making the proper connections, we can better appreciate and comprehend Yahowah. He is *nagad* | conspicuously providing the information we need, expounding upon the Word of God, so that we are prepared to respond.

When it comes to Yahowah and His testimony we all have a choice. We can stand with Him, present and accounted for, or we can reject Him and cling to the words of men like Paul, Akiba, and Muhammad, instead. We can do as the rabbis and the Roman Catholic Church have done and render *bayn* as "between," thereby inferring that ordinary men and women like you and me cannot approach God on our own and, therefore, need someone to intervene for us. Or we can expound upon the primary meaning of *bayn*, which is to understand, and then espouse its virtues. It's now your choice because I've made mine.

In this regard, so long as we are comfortable approaching Yahowah and are willing to examine and consider His testimony for ourselves, there is nothing wrong with listening to and benefiting from someone like Moseh, learning from a man who devoted much of his life to accurately quoting and then insightfully commenting upon Yahowah's instructions. It is the very reason that Yahowah chose to communicate through men like him. It is the express reason *Dabarym*, which is Moseh's recital and commentary on the Towrah, was added to the Towrah, becoming its fifth book.

Yahowah spoke to all who would listen to Him. His words are available for everyone to study. Throughout His Towrah and Prophets God addresses us in first person. And yet, we do not have to approach His testimony alone – translating it ourselves – or do the research to *bayn* | understand everything independently. Yahowah did not work alone, nor should we. *Moseh* | Moses served as a guide, illuminating the way to form a relationship with Yahowah. So did *Dowd* | David throughout the *Mizmowr wa Mashal* | Psalms and Proverbs. We are Family.

While the last time Yahowah spoke to us publicly through one of His prophets was 2,450 years ago, He has not forgotten His people nor His promise to them. He still wants to communicate with them, to guide and teach them. It is not that He has anything additional to say, it is just that He wants His people to listen to what He has already revealed. That is one of many reasons I have devoted the time to study on your behalf, to assist you, translating His words into the *lingua franca* of our time, all while sharing insights I have been shown by closely examining and carefully considering what God revealed through prophets like Moseh and Dowd, Yasha'yah and Yirma'yah.

Frankly, I do not understand why anyone in their right mind would be afraid of Yahowah. But evidently, the Children of Yisra'el were uncomfortable in His presence…

"And yet (*ky* – but by contrast, indeed)**, you, rather than respect and revere the profound and awesome appearance of the fire, at the moment, you may be frightened by the presence of the flames** (*yare' min paneh ha 'esh* – you may be nervous and anxious, a bit timid to face the glowing light and energy (qal perfect))**.**

And so (*wa*)**, you have not ascended** (*'alah* – you have not climbed or gone up (qal perfect)) **into the mountain** (*ba ha har*) **for the declaration** (*la 'amar* – toward the statement, and for Him to say (qal infinitive))**:…"** (*Dabarym* 5:5)

While I do not concur, I suspect most people find God not to their liking. If this were not true, why else would men and women conceive and worship so many fakes? The fact is, God shares little in common with most people because He is not religious or political, patriotic or conspiratorial, flexible or tolerant, soft-spoken or accommodating.

They feared what they should have revered. It precluded them from ascending into the very presence of Yah.

That known, based upon all we have learned, it is clearly wonderful next to the fire, warm and inviting. Come, sit next to our Heavenly Father, and listen…

"'**I am** (*'anky*) **Yahowah** (𐤉𐤄𐤅𐤄 – YaHoWaH; from *y-hayah* – I was, I am, and I will always be)**, your God** (*'elohym 'atah* – your shepherd, a ram among the sheep, and the doorway to an expansive and abundant life for those who are engaged, standing up, reaching up, and looking up (suffixed in the second-person singular making this introduction personal))**, who relationally and beneficially** (*'asher* – who to show the correct and narrow path to get the most out of life) **brought you out and delivered you** (*yatsa' 'atah* – descended to serve you individually in this moment in time, extending Myself to guide you (singular, and thus personally), doing everything which is required to lead and withdraw you, such that you would respond to Me, becoming more like Me in the process, disseminating the information you need publicly and openly so as to direct you individually (hifil perfect – at a moment in time God engaged with us in such a way that we were empowered to come out)) **away from the realm** (*min 'erets* – out of the land, region, territory, nation, and country) **of the Crucibles of Religious and Political Oppression** (*Mitsraym* – of the cauldrons of governmental, military, economic, and conspiratorial coercion and cruelty, where the people were confined, restricted, and persecuted; plural of *matsowr* – to be treated as a foe and besieged during a time of testing and tribulation; from *tsuwr* – to be bound and constrained by an adversary, besieged and assaulted, as if in a concentration camp by those showing great hostility)**, out of the house** (*min beyth* – from the home, household, family, and place) **of slavery and servitude** (*'ebed* – of bondage and working for one's salvation, of being under the control of government authorities and religious officials)." (*Dabarym* 5:6)

Everyone in this audience knew this, because they had personally experienced it, and they were witnesses to the many miracles and close encounters of a personal kind. Therefore, this was not written for those listening to Moseh on this day – but instead for us.

As a result, I would like to offer my two shekels for the reason that it was stated here and then repeated in the Shabat presentation. First, Yahowah wants us to know that He is not a Lord who oppresses but instead a Father who embraces. His words, His Towrah, liberate. It is an essential truth which has been obscured by Rabbinic Law and Pauline Doctrine.

Second, this was not the first, nor will it be the last *Yatsa'* | Exodus. Most notably, there is another on our horizon – one in which Yahowah will use His words to escort His people out of the three Babylons. If you want to exist in His presence, be prepared to go home.

"You will not continue to exist with (*lo' hayah la 'atah* – you shall not be, neither function nor move toward, arise, live, nor appear, drawing near if you *lo' hayah* | negate the basis and existence of My name, Yahowah, which will cause you to *lo' hayah* – no longer exist with (qal imperfect – continually and literally)) **other** (*'acher* – following someone else's, different, extra, another, or additional) **gods** (*'elohym*) **over and above** (*'al* – elevated beyond, in proximity to or near, before, or in addition to) **My presence** (*paneh 'any* – My appearance or face, My proximity or identity)." (*Dabarym* 5:7)

Dabarym / Deuteronomy 5:6-7 is word for word as Yahowah presents the initial statement in *Shemowth* / Exodus 20: 2-3. It is the Word of our God.

The lone prerequisite of the Covenant is to walk away from Babel, from the mixing together and commingling of confounding religious and political mythology, which is precisely what God has asked us to do here at the conclusion of the First Statement and throughout the Second. As a result, it is astonishing that the vast preponderance of people not only continues to be religious, but that most have one or more religious objects in their possession.

What follows in *Dabarym* 5:8, 9, 10, and 11 is also identical to what we read in *Shemowth* 20:4, 5, and 6…

"You should not continue to act on behalf of or associate yourself with (*lo' 'asah la 'atah* – you should not make a practice of attending to or doing anything with, you should not approach, act upon, or engage with, you should not assign on your behalf any function or purpose to, you should not fashion nor profit from, you should not conceive, acquire, celebrate, or work around nor near (qal imperfect – conveying a literal interpretation and ongoing actions and unfolding consequences)) **a religious image or object of worship** (*pesel* – a shaped, sculpted, carved, cast, chiseled, or designed icon or idol associated with the divine, a representation of a god)**, or any** (*wa kol* – nor any kind or variation of a [*wa* is from 4QDeut]) **visual or formed representation of something** (*tamunah* – likeness, appearance, idiom, association, or appearance, in a shape or form which depicts or resembles and attempts to establish a relationship by way of a substitution; from *myn* – a living species or ancestor)**, which by association is** (*'asher* – which to show that the correct path is narrow and restrictive) **in** (*ba*) **the heavens above** (*ha shamaym min ma'al* – the spiritual realm on high including the sun, moon, planets, and stars above)**, or** (*wa*) **is related to that which is** (*'asher*) **on** (*ba*) **the earth** (*ha 'erets* – land and ground) **below** (*min tahath*)**, or** (*wa*) **found in connection** (*'asher*) **with** (*ba*) **the waters** (*ha maym*) **beneath the land** (*min tahath la ha 'erets* – from below the ground)**.** (*Dabarym* 5:8)

You should not speak about them on your own initiative or make a practice of bowing down and worshiping them (*lo' chawah la hem* – you should not continue to promote their message on your own accord or display their words because such uncoerced and ongoing verbal declarations and announcements will influence you, you should not religiously prostrate yourself in obeisance and homage to them, show any allegiance to them on an ongoing basis, or habitually worship them, especially if not compelled or forced to make confessions (hitpael imperfect jussive – acting without any compulsion, habitually or continually responding to the will of the religious influences)), **and** (*wa*) **you shall not habitually serve them or compel anyone to worship them** (*lo' 'abad hem* – you should not continually work or labor in their cause or make a career of working as their ministers, you should not submit to them in servitude or encourage anyone else to do so, neither should you act upon them nor consistently engage with them (hofal imperfect – you should not make a habit of forcing, encouraging, nor compelling anyone to act or serve on their behalf)).

For, indeed (*ky* – because and emphasizing this point), **I** (*'anky*), **Yahowah** (*Yahowah* – as directed in His *towrah* – teaching regarding His *hayah* – existence), **your God** (*'elohy 'atah*), **am a fiercely protective and emotionally devoted God, a steadfastly loyal and jealous God** (*qana' 'el* – a God who is desirous of exclusivity in a deeply loving and committed relationship, a God who is emotionally passionate and extremely defensive of those He zealously loves, a God who goes above and beyond to acquire His creation so as to bring forth new life), **actually counting and reckoning** (*paqad* – literally taking stock of and genuinely recording, assigning, and depositing (qal participle – a descriptive verb with literal implications)) **the perversity of twisting and distorting** (*'awon* – the depravity of perverting and manipulating, deviating from the way, the guilt and punishment derived from delusion and depravity, the liability for unfaithfulness and wrongdoing) **of the fathers** (*'ab* – of parents) **onto** (*'al*) **the children** (*ben* – sons) **to** (*'el* – unto [from 4QDeut]) **the third and the fourth generations** (*shileshym wa 'al ribea'*) **of those who are averse to Me** (*sane' 'any* – of those who are openly hostile and dislike Me, who abhor, hate, detest, and loathe Me, literally striving maliciously against Me, shunning Me by refusing to engage in a relationship with Me (qal participle – serving as a literal and vivid depiction as a verbal adjective)). (*Dabarym* 5:9)

However, I genuinely act and actually engage to literally prepare, perform, and produce (*'asah* – I actively effect and appoint, offering and celebrating, even demonstrating by doing what is required to deliver on behalf of those who respond (qal participle)) **unfailing mercy, unearned favor, and genuine kindness** (*chesed* – actual forgiveness, steadfast and ardent appreciation, a friendly and affectionate relationship, faithfulness and goodness, loyal and devoted love) **on behalf of** (*la'* – to enable the approach of) **the thousands** (*'elephym*) **who move toward Me and love Me** (*la 'ahab 'any* – who form a close and affectionate, loving and friendly, familial relationship with Me, coming to know and like Me, who come to prefer Me and find an association with Me desirable) **and also** (*wa* – in addition) **who approach Me by closely examining and carefully considering** (*la shamar* – who enter My presence by becoming observant and actually focusing upon, thoroughly scrutinizing and thoughtfully evaluating (qal participle)) **My instructions and directions, My terms and conditions** (*mitswah 'any* – the verbal and written stipulations, statements, and structure which uphold My Covenant, My authoritative guidelines and codicils which serve as prescriptions for My relationship agreement and mutually binding contract; a compound of *ma* – to ponder the who, what, why, when, where, and how questions regarding God's *tsawah* – authorized and authoritative communications, appointed and ordained mission and leadership)." (*Dabarym* 5:10)

Clearly, Yahowah does not want His people to be religious. He does not want us anywhere around this plague of death.

Once again, what follows in *Dabarym* 5:11 mirrors the testimony found in *Shemowth* 20:7. With so much at stake, this is reassuring to those of us who have come to know and love Yahowah's name…

"'You should not continue to deceive, nor should you tolerate or support delusions (*lo' nasha'* – you should not habitually deploy or advance clever tricks to enrich yourself by indebting others, and you should avoid beguiling people on an ongoing basis by consistently lifting up, promoting, or forgiving that which causes them to miss the way by forgetting something (qal imperfect)) **associated with** (*'eth* – through or by way of the) **the name and reputation** (*shem* – the renown and proper designation) **of Yahowah** (*Yahowah* – the proper pronunciation of YaHoWaH, our *'elowah* – God as directed in His *ToWRaH* – teaching regarding His *HaYaH* – existence and our *ShaLoWM* – restoration), **your God** (*'elohym*), **thereby negating the value of My name by advancing worthless and lifeless deceptions** (*la ha showa'* (errantly transliterated *shav'*) – deploying that which advances devastating dishonesty, nullifying one's existence, leading to emptiness and nothingness, so as to advance deceitful and lifeless lies which are ineffectual, futile, and ruinous).

For, indeed (*ky* – because), **Yahowah** (*Yahowah* – written as directed by His *towrah* – teaching) **will not forgive or leave unpunished** (*lo' naqah* – as an ongoing admonition unconstrained by time, He will not purify nor pardon, He will not acquit nor free from guilt, He will not exempt from judgment or sentencing, nor will He consider innocent nor release (piel imperfect)) **those who** (*'eth 'asher* – in association with others) **consistently deceive, actually beguile, and habitually delude, promote or accept trickery so as to negate** (*nasha'* – religiously using deception to continually mislead, lifting up and advancing a clever, albeit dishonest, ruse (qal imperfect)) **an**

108

association with (*'eth* – through) **His name** (*shem* – renown, reputation, and proper designation) **such that it diminishes its value, including ineffectual lies which lead to lifelessness, nullifying one's existence** (*la ha showa'* – devastating deceptions which destroy, leading to emptiness, worthlessness, and nothingness, futilely deceiving in a ruinous manner).'" (*Dabarym* 5:11)

The very thing religious men and women have consistently done over the past three thousand years is precisely what God asked us not to do, saying that it was unforgivable. Religious individuals and institutions negated the value of Yahowah's name by deliberately editing it out of His testimony seven thousand times and replacing it with the satanic title: "Lord." If you do not know and use Yahowah's name, if you are complacent around those who refer to Him by other names, you do not know Him and He does not know you.

Thus concludes Moseh's presentation of what Yahowah inscribed on the First of the second set of Two Tablets. His declaration not only affirmed what we learned by translating these Statements the first time they were presented, but we are also now blessed with an early 1st-century parchment confirming what was shared on this day circa 1447 BCE. Moreover, Moseh's preamble conveyed his mindset – which was to encourage understanding.

From this point on, however, something changes and not by a little but by a lot. Some might claim that the second edition (remember the first set of Tablets were shattered) of the Second Tablet is so different than the one recorded in *Shemowth* / Exodus 20 that Moseh must have written it down incorrectly. And yet, that is not how I perceive them because there are no contradictions, only amplifications and explanations.

In *Shemowth* / Exodus 20, I think Yahowah recited what He inscribed on the first edition of the Second Tablet.

Then in *Dabarym* / Deuteronomy 5, I think Moseh expounded upon Yahowah's Instructions to the Children of Yisra'el in the hope that more would appreciate their relevance and purpose. This is especially true regarding the nature of the Shabat and the concept behind valuing our Father and Mother. Doing this very thing, explaining the Towrah so that we would know how to observe it, is God's purpose and Moseh's mission.

In what follows, we are confronted with not one, but two instances of "*shamar* – observe," indicating that we are being told explicitly to "closely examine and carefully consider" "'*eth ha Shabat* – that which is associated with the promise of the seventh day." It should be "*la qadash* – set apart from other days and thus be special" "*ka 'asher* – with regard to its purpose, which is to show the way to the benefits of the relationship and for the express reason of its comparative symbolism which is designed to reveal the correct and straightforward path to walk to get the greatest joy out of life."

God's next two statements in *Dabarym* 5:12 are similar, but not exactly the same as what He revealed in *Shemowth*. For example, Shemowth 20:8 begins with *zakar* | remember while Dabarym 5:12 reads *shamar* | observe. These are related concepts, whereby doing one will lead to the other. Further, *Dabarym* adds "*tsawah 'atah* – to instruct you" to the text, demonstrating the purpose of the Shabat.

Then as we approach the conclusion of *Dabarym* 5:14, either Moseh or Yahowah, perhaps both, add something by way of an explanation that was not provided in *Shemowth* 20. Further, by the time we approach *Dabarym* 5:15, Yahowah is once again being presented as the One who liberates us from the Crucibles of Religious and Political Subjugation. This is important because rather than the Seventh Day being a time of idle inactivity, of doing nothing, it is now a special celebration for observing how the Strong Arm of Yahowah separates us from the harmful aspects of man's counterproductive ways. It is now a loud and unmistakable call to come home.

"**Observe** (*shamar* – closely examine and carefully consider (qal infinitive absolute)) **that which is associated with the day of the Shabat** (*'eth ha yowm ha shabat* – the purpose of the seventh day, the period of reflection at the end of the week, reminiscent of the promise of settling debts so we can settle down by observing the oath in association with this means to satisfy and enrich; from *shaba'* – fulfilling and satisfying the promise of seven to abundantly empower and enrich) **so as to keep it set apart** (*la qadash huw'* – such that it remains separate and distinct unto Him for purifying and cleansing and thus special to approach Him (piel stem – where the object, Yahowah, is engaged and acts in response to the subject's (our) willingness to set this day apart and infinitive construct – serving as a verbal noun)), **consistent with its purpose, which is to show the way to the benefits of the relationship as** (*ka 'asher* – for the express reason of its comparative symbolism which is designed to reveal the correct and straightforward path to walk to get the greatest joy out of life as) **Yahowah** (*YaHoWaH* – an accurate presentation of the name of *'elowah* – God as guided by His *towrah* – instructions regarding His *hayah* – existence), **your God** (*'elohy 'atah*), **instructed you** (*tsawah 'atah* – directed you, appointing and ordaining for you (piel perfect))." (*Dabarym* 5:12)

With the differences between *zakar* and *shamar* duly noted, and the addition of *tsawah* fully appreciated, what follows in *Dabarym* 5:13 is consistent with what we read in *Shemowth* 20:9...

Six (*shesh* – speaking of that which is bleached white or adorned in fine linen) **days** (*yowmym* – periods of time) **you should actually and continuously work** (*'abad* – you should engage in ongoing labor, working for oneself or for another, expending the energy to be productive at your job (qal stem – denoting a literal interpretation and imperfect conjugation – which speaks of that which is ongoing)), **and** (*wa*) **choose to act, engaging in** (*'asah* – express your own freewill to prepare and accomplish what you can do at that time, capitalizing upon and advancing, doing and profiting for this brief time from (qal stem – addresses genuine relationships, perfect conjugation – denoting actions which are complete and have been accomplished at some point in time, and consecutive mood – conveying volition)) **all** (*kol* – the entirety of) **your service as a spiritual messenger and with the** *Mala'kah* | **Spiritual Messenger** (*mala'kah 'atah* – your usefulness communicating as a Godly implement, working on behalf of the feminine manifestation of the Heavenly Representative, making informative announcements as a witness on behalf of the Spiritual Counselor; feminine form of *mal'ak* – heavenly messenger). (*Dabarym* 5:13)

But (*wa*) **the seventh** (*shabyi'y* – the solemn promise which fulfills and satisfies, abundantly enriching those who listen and are observant of the role of the seventh; from *shaba'* – to take an oath and make a sworn promise to fulfill, completely satisfying, providing an abundance of enriching benefits) **day** (*yowm* – period of time), **the Shabat** (*ha shabat* – the seventh day, the period of reflection at the end of the week, reminiscent of the promise of settling debts so we can settle down by observing the oath of association; from *shaba'* – fulfilling and satisfying the promise of seven to abundantly empower and enrich), **is to approach** (*la* – is for drawing near, associating with and moving toward) **Yahowah** (𐤉𐤄𐤅𐤄 – a transliteration of *YaHoWaH* as instructed in His *towrah* – teaching regarding His *hayah* – existence), **your God** (*'elohym 'atah*).

On it (*'al hy'* – during it [from 4QDeut]), **you should not continuously engage in** (*lo' 'asah* – you should not habitually act out, consistently preparing or producing, nor should you try to actually fashion, accomplish, or constantly do (qal stem imperfect conjugation)) **all of** (*kol*) **the work of the *Mala'kah* | Heavenly Messenger and Spiritual Counselor** (*Mala'kah* – the service of God's Implement, Envoy, and Witness, the Ministry and Mission of God's spiritual manifestation; feminine of *mal'ak* – heavenly messenger and spiritual representative) **yourself** (*'atah*)**, your son** (*ben*)**, your daughter** (*bat*)**, your male and female servants and staff** (*'ebed wa 'amah* – your employees and those men and women who work for and with you)**, your means of production** (*behemah* – your animals and beasts of burden) **as well as** (*wa*) **those visitors** (*ger* – foreigners) **who relationally** (*'asher*) **are in your home or on your property** (*ba sha'ar* – are inside your doors or gates; from *sha'ar* – to think and be reasonable)**, so that** (*lama'an* – for the reason, intent, and purpose) **your male and female employees** (*'ebed wa 'amah* – your staff and servants, those men and women who work for and with you)**, as well as you** (*kamow 'atah* – like you, similarly and simultaneously along with you) **may be restored spiritually** (*nuwach* – may be reenergized spiritually; from *ruwach* – spirit (qal imperfect))**.**" (*Dabarym* 5:14)

The differences between *Shemowth* 20:10 and *Dabarym* 5:14 begin with "*'al hy'* – on it." And then in Moseh's presentation, the prophet adds "*lama'an 'ebed wa 'amah kamow 'atah nuwach* – so that you and your employees may be spiritually reenergized and restored."

Moseh continues to elaborate, explaining the purpose of the Shabat, in the following words, all of which are true, but none of which are found in the *Shemowth* 20 edition of the Second Tablet...

"**In addition** (*wa*)**, you should remember** (*zakar* – call to mind, recollect, mention, and proclaim (qal perfect)) **that, indeed** (*ky*)**, you were** (*hayah* – you existed as (qal perfect)) **a slave** (*'ebed* – a servant owned by another) **in the land** (*ba 'erets* – in the realm and country) **of the Crucibles of Political and Religious Oppression** (*Mitsraym* – the cauldrons of military, economic, conspiratorial, societal, and governmental persecution and subjugation; plural of *matsowr* – to be considered inferior and besieged during a time of testing and tribulation, from *tsuwr* – to be bound and confined by an adversary, assaulted, shut up, and enclosed as if in a concentration camp by those showing great hostility) **when** (*wa* – and so) **Yahowah** (*YaHoWaH* – an accurate presentation of the name of *'elowah* – God as guided by His *towrah* – instructions regarding His *hayah* – existence)**, your God** (*'elohy 'atah*)**, brought you out, withdrawing you** (*yatsa' 'atah* – descended and extended Himself, came forth to lead and deliver you, taking you (hifil imperfect)) **from there** (*min sham | shem* – out of and away from that place called by this name and having that reputation) **with** (*ba* – by and in) **a mighty and firm, powerful and protective** (*chazaq* – very strong and influential, extraordinarily capable and intensely prepared, resolutely passionate and encouraging, assertive and aggressive, feisty and steadfast) **hand** (*yad* – ability to accomplish the task at hand, representing the first letter in Yah's name which as an open hand reaching down and out)**, and with** (*wa ba*) **the Zarowa' | Productive Shepherd and Strong Arm** (*Zarowa'* – the prevailing and effective nature of a shepherd, the strength, resolve, and overall ability of a remarkably important and impactful individual of action who, as a leader and fighter is engaged as a shepherd among his sheep, who is fruitful in his ways, accomplishing the mission, especially when sowing the seeds of truth while denoting and advancing the purpose of the arm of God, of His shepherd and sacrificial lamb) **having been extended** (*natah* – outstretched and reaching out).

114

For this reason (*'al ken* – upon these grounds above all others, it is right, therefore, that)**, Yahowah** (*YaHoWaH*)**, your God** (*'elohy 'atah*)**, instructed you** (*tsawah 'atah* – directed you (piel perfect)) **to approach by observing** (*la shamar* – to move toward by closely examining and carefully considering (qal infinitive construct – a literal descriptive verb and genuinely actionable noun) [from 1QDeut]) **that which is associated with the day** (*'eth yowm*) **of the Shabat** (*ha shabat* – the seventh day, the period of reflection at the end of the week, reminiscent of the promise of settling debts so we can settle down by observing the oath of association; from *shaba'* – fulfilling and satisfying the promise of seven to abundantly empower and enrich) **so that it is set apart and special** (*'eth qodesh* – so that it is uncommon, cleansing, and perfecting [from 1QDeut])**.**" (*Dabarym* 5:15)

Yahowah is reinforcing a misunderstood aspect of His nature and plan – that of Him being our liberator, the One freeing us from the propensity of mankind to oppress, persecute, and subjugate through religion and politics. It is religious and political institutions which strive to control and militant and patriotic individuals who seek obedience and compliance.

Moseh explains, just as Yahowah did with 'Abraham, withdrawing him from *Babel* | Babylon before establishing the *Beryth* | Covenant, and then did for the Children of Yisra'el, removing them from *Mitsraym* | Religious and Political Oppression prior to bequeathing His *Towrah* | Teaching, that He is offering to do the same for us. And therefore, the Shabat exists as a time to celebrate Yahowah's powerful and protective, firm and resolute, hand reaching out to lift us up and take us home.

And if that were not enough to make your eyes sparkle and your mind tingle, Moseh introduces us to the role the *Zarowa'* play in Yahowah's plan to free His children from religion so that we might engage in the relationship. There are three Zarowa', two great and one small. Moseh serves as the Productive Shepherd while Dowd is the Protective Ram and Sacrificial Lamb, both vociferously sowing the seeds of truth.

And then because we are on the cusp of the Great Celebration of the Shabat and, thus, of a Second *Yatsa'* | Exodus, there would be a third *zarowa'*, the little *z*, who would use the words and deeds of the *Chazaq Zarowa'* to call Yisra'el and Yahuwdah back home to Yah. And so, as Moseh affirms, this is the reason behind Yahowah's *tsawah* | instructions on how to properly *shamar* | observe the *Shabat* | celebration of the Seventh Day such that it remains *qodesh* | special.

Following this amazingly insightful explanation of the Shabat in *Dabarym* 5, Moseh's testimony once again mirrors the *Shemowth* 20 presentation…

"For (*ky*) **in six** (*shesh* – symbolic of mankind being bleached white and purified on the sixth) **days** (*yowmym*), **Yahowah** (*YaHoWaH* – an accurate presentation of the name of our *'elowah* – God as guided by His *towrah* – instructions regarding His *hayah* – existence) **acted and engaged, preparing and producing everything associated with completing** (*'asah* – totally fashioning, instituting, advancing, accomplishing, doing, celebrating, and attending to the full extent of (qal stem perfect conjugation)) **the heavens** (*'eth ha shamaym* – the spiritual realm), **and the earth** (*wa ha 'erets* – the material world), **and the waters** (*wa ha yam*), **as well as all** (*kol* – everything) **which relationally** (*'asher*) **is in them** (*ba*). **And then** (*wa*), **He became completely settled spiritually** (*nuwach* – He resolved every remaining issue, satisfying, appeasing, and conciliating by way of the Spirit (*nuwach* is related to *ruwach* – spirit)) **during** (*ba*) **the Almighty's seventh** (*ha shaby'y 'al* – God's solemn promise which fulfills and satisfies those who listen and are observant of the role of the oath of the seventh) **day** (*yowm*).

Therefore (*ken* – consequently, this is true and correct)**, Yahowah** (𐤉𐤄𐤅𐤄 – the pronunciation of *YaHoWaH*) **blessed and adored** (*barak* – knelt down and lowered Himself, offering a greeting along with an opportunity to meet, favoring (piel perfect)) **everything associated with this day** (*'eth ha yowm*)**, the Shabat** (*ha shabat* – the seventh day, the period to reflect on the enriching nature of the relationship at the end of the week, reminiscent of the promise of settling debts so we can settle down by observing the oath of association; from *shaba'* – fulfilling and satisfying the promise of seven to abundantly empower and enrich)**, setting it apart** (*qodesh* – separating it from that which is common, ordinary, and popular, making it special, dedicating it to separation, cleansing, and purifying)**."** (*Dabarym* 5: after 15 and before 16 from 1QDeut4)

Moseh's presentation of the Second of Seven Instructions on the Second of Two Tablets is identical to that of Shemowth 20 with two exceptions. The first is the addition of "*ka 'asher* – consistent with these metaphorical comparisons showing the way to the benefits of the relationship." And the second uses *wa le'ma'an yatab la 'atah* to explain these accounts and comparisons providing us with the ability to prosper when we are right with God.

"You should choose to carefully consider, view as worthy, enormously valuable, extremely significant, and highly enriching (*kabed* – of your own volition elect to distinguish, respect, esteem, and honor, perceiving as awesomely impressive, tremendously relevant, extremely great, and extraordinarily important, even glorious so as to be abundantly enriched and empowered to a very high degree (written in the piel stem revealing that our Heavenly Father and Spiritual Mother are influenced by and respond to our perceptions of them, and in the imperative mood which expresses either a command, an intent, or an exhortation in the second person which is subject to volition)), **accordingly, the symbolism of** (*'eth* – that which is represented by and in accord with; from *'owth* – as a miraculous sign and distinguishing symbol based upon your consent to an agreement with) **your Father** (*'ab 'atah* – biological, adoptive, or heavenly father) **and** (*wa*) **that which is represented by your** (*'eth* – that which is represented by and in accord with; from *'owth* – as a miraculous sign and distinguishing symbol based upon your consent to an agreement with) **Mother** (*'em 'atah* – biological, adoptive, or spiritual mother) **consistent with these metaphorical comparisons showing the way to the benefits of the relationship which are representative of how** (*ka 'asher* – revealing the correct path to walk to give meaning to life by making comparisons and connections by which) **Yahowah** (*Yahowah* – as directed in His *towrah* – teaching regarding His *hayah* – existence), **your God** (*'elohym 'atah*), **instructed you** (*tsawah 'atah* – directed you, proposing for you (piel perfect)).

As a result, and through the intent of these associations (*le'ma'an* – so that consistent with the purpose of these comparisons, allegories, and similitudes), **your days** (*yowmym 'atah*) **will be continuously lengthened** (*'arak* – will be elongated and always prolonged, growing and continuing in harmony with My will (written in the hifil stem, imperfect conjugation, and paragogic nun ending which, like the cohortative, expresses volition in the first person)), **thereby achieving the purpose of this statement which is that** (*wa le'ma'an* – so that based upon these accounts and comparisons, as well as their approach and intent) **you will do well, be successful, and prosper by being right** (*yatab la 'atah* – it will be best for you to be thorough and correct, effectively engaged, performing appropriately, and living joyfully in a pleasing and agreeable manner) **upon** (*'al* – on the) **the earth** (*ha 'adamah* – the ground or land; feminine of *'adam* the name of the first man created in God's image with a *neshamah* – conscience) **which**

relationally and as a blessing (*'asher* – to reveal the narrow, correct, beneficial, joyful, and straightforward steps to walk along the path to get the most out of life) **Yahowah** (*Yahowah* – the proper pronunciation of YaHoWaH, our *'elowah* – God as directed in His *ToWRaH* – teaching regarding His *HaYaH* – existence and our *ShaLoWM* – restoration), **your God** (*'elohym 'atah*), **is actually giving to you** (*nathan la 'atah* – is literally producing, providing, allowing, granting, and genuinely bestowing to you as a gift and for you to approach and draw near (qal participle))." (*Dabarym* 5:16)

As I have mentioned, it is wonderful to see *ka 'asher* inserted into the text because it says that we should consider the "comparative and metaphorical associations which lead us to correctly assessing the path to the benefits of the relationship and to get the most out of life." Similarly, God's next phrase, "*le'ma'an yatab la 'atah* – thereby obtaining the purpose of this statement which is that you will do well, be successful, and prosper by being right," also validates our metaphorical and spiritual approach to understanding. Therefore, Yahowah wants us to interpret His revelation as we have been doing.

The remaining five Instructions are readily understood and interpreted from both a physical and spiritual perspective. And they are essentially unchanged from their previous portrayal.

"'You should not kill on an ongoing basis (*lo' ratsach* – you should not make a practice of taking the life of another whether by accident, revenge, manslaughter, premeditation, assassination, governmental execution, military slaughter, or murder (qal imperfect) [there is no *wa* in 4QDeut but there is in the MT]). (*Dabarym* 5:17)

You should not continue to participate in idolatrous worship or make a habit of taking another's wife (*lo' na'aph* – you should not be unfaithful by being religious and pursuing other gods or have sexual relations with a married woman [there is no *wa* in 4QDeut]). (*Dabarym* 5:18)

You should not make a habit of stealing (*lo' ganab* – you should not routinely take something from others without their permission, neither kidnap nor commit robbery using deception or acting secretly [there is no *wa* in 4QDeut]). (*Dabarym* 5:19)

You should not continuously answer and respond (*lo' 'anah* – you should refrain from replying by providing testimony or consistently making a declaration [there is no *wa* in 4QDeut]) **in conjunction with** (*ba*) **your neighbor's evil thoughts** (*rea' 'atah* – the sinful and improper, regretful and debilitating way of your countrymen, friends, companions, or associates) **as a deceptive or misleading** (*seqer* – false, conniving, clever, mistaken, vain, or unreliable, lying or fraudulent, useless or irrelevant) **witness** (*'ed* – source of evidence by way of testimony). (*Dabarym* 5:20)

You should not make a practice out of coveting (*lo' chamad* – you should not habitually desire, delighting in, lusting for, craving, nor seek pleasure from (qal imperfect)) **your neighbor's** (*rea' 'atah* – your countryman's, friend's, companion's, or associate's inappropriate behavior and improper opinions, nor the sadness seen in their) **home or household** (*beyth* – family or house).

You should not continuously covet (*lo' chamad* – you should not desire, lust for, crave, nor seek pleasure from on an ongoing basis (qal imperfect)) **your improper neighbor's** (*rea' 'atah* – your countryman's, friend's, companion's, or associate's inappropriate behavior with, their misguided opinions regarding, nor the sadness seen in their) **wife or woman** (*'ishah* – of an individual female, of maternal flames, or as Gefilte fish flambé), **or** (*wa*) **his male or female servants** (*'ebed huw' wa 'amah huw'* – his employees or officials, the working men and women serving him), **his comings and goings or his domesticated animals** (*sowr huw' wa chamowr huw'* – that which is capable of providing mobility and bearing a load, carrying cargo, his material assets, his belongings and possessions, means of transport, food, and production, namely his cattle or donkeys), **or anything** (*wa kol*) **which is associated** (*'asher*) **with** (*la* – regarding) **your maligned countryman's errant opinions or inappropriate behavior** (*rea' 'atah* – your friend's, companion's, or associate's disconcerting thoughts, evil principles, or shameful ways).'" (*Dabarym* 5:21)

The Instructions and their implications properly conveyed, Moseh shared these concluding thoughts…

"These are the words (*'eth ha dabar ha 'eleh* – these specifically are the statements) **Yahowah** (*Yahowah* – written as directed by His *towrah* – teaching) **communicated** (*dabar* – spoke and expressed at that time (piel perfect)) **to** (*'el*) **everyone** (*kol* – the entire and whole) **of you assembled** (*qahal 'atah* – of your gathering together, your contingent and community) **beside** (*ba*) **the mountain** (*ha har* – the high and elevated ridgeline), **from** (*min* – out of) **the midst** (*tawek*) **of the fire and light** (*'esh* – of radiant energy and brilliant flames) **reduced in magnitude** (*choshek* – so as to obscure Himself by reducing the extent of His light [from 4QDeut]) **by the dense water-laden** (*wa ha 'araphel* – as well as the thick) **cloud** (*'anan*) **with a great and powerful** (*gadowl* – substantial and magnificent, important and distinguished, even glorious) **voice** (*qowl*).

He did not add anything more (*wa lo' yasaph*). **And** (*wa*) **He wrote them, engraving them** (*kathab hem* – He inscribed them using alphabetic letters to form written words) **on** (*'al*) **Two** (*shanaym*) **Tablets** (*luwach* – slabs, tables, or plates suitable for chiseling and inscribing words) **of Stone** (*'eben* – solid rock). **Then, He gave them** (*wa* *nathan hem* – He prepared, produces, and handed them as a gift) **to me** (*'el 'any* – as God to myself)." (*Dabarym* / Words / Deuteronomy 5:22)

If you are a religious Jew steeped in the Oral Law of Rabbis Akiba and Maimonides, a Christian immersed in the poison of Pauline Doctrine, a Muslim misled by Muhammad, or a Mormon deceived by Joseph Smith, take note: "He did not add anything more."

You now know that the overwhelming preponderance of the religious textual changes, especially the additions and deletions, the corruptions and counterfeits, of Yahowah's Word, were not authorized by God. Each perversion, including the religious nomenclature, preached by the religious is erroneous, notably the words, concepts, titles, and names: Commandment, Law, Bible, Old Testament, and Lord to name but a few.

I was not the first, nor will I be the last, to realize the pagan nature of these corruptions. Upon sharing the initial insights revealed in *Yada Yahowah* with America's most famous protestant preacher at the time, Jerry Falwell replied, "Everything you have asserted is true, but if I were to say these things, I would lose my followers and their funding. And if you say these things to them, they will label you a kook."

The truth has never been popular. So those willing to share it are assailed by the men and women who benefit from all manner of deceptions. In fact, when you share what you have discovered in these pages, your religious friends will turn against you. Unable to refute anything you have to say with evidence or reason, pastors, priests, and rabbis, even family members, will resort to character assassination.

While I openly acknowledge the inadvertent inaccuracy on my part, if you were of the belief that your favorite English "Bible" represents the perfect, complete, and inerrant word of God, or even that God's name is "God," or that He called His revelation the "Bible," you are now confronted with a choice. You will either disregard Yah's witness as it is presented in this *Introduction to God*, *Yada Yahowah*, *Observations*, and *Coming Home* and remain naive, or you will use the tools and insights you have been given to become observant, awakened to a far more glorious reality.

If you dare go on, and venture out in pursuit of knowing Yahowah better, you will discover countless affirmations that almost everything Yahowah has to say conflicts with the sermons, teachings, dogmas, and schemes of religious, political, and military leaders, academicians, pastors, popes, priests, and rabbis. No institution is immune. No religion is believable. No political party is just. No nation is worthy. No man is credible.

Now regarding my own *mea culpas*: there were seven mistakes in the *Yada Yahowah* Series which I have endeavored to edit out of the 35 volumes. It was not until after I had compiled the first edition of *Yada Yahowah* that I came to realize that Paul was a false prophet. Should you be interested in the evidence against Sha'uwl (Paul's actual name), I invite you to read the five volumes which now comprise *Twistianity*, available free at *www.YadaYah.com* or in printed form at Amazon.com. As a result of this very unpopular and, indeed, surprising discovery, I now have striven to present Paul's letters as Yahowah sees them – as the Plague of Death.

Second, while studying *Yirma'yah* / Jeremiah 31, I discovered that the Covenant has not yet been renewed. We know this because, when the Covenant is renewed, Yahowah's Towrah will be placed inside of us to guide us throughout eternity. Yahowah's message has not changed. God is not capricious. He has not eliminated or added anything. This then leads to the recognition that the Christian New Testament is neither inspired nor credible.

Third, Dowd is the Passover Lamb. There was no "Jesus" and no "Christ." There is no basis for "Christians," "Church," a virgin birth, the cross, a resurrection, Christmas, or Easter. Further, there isn't a single prophecy in which "Jesus" is named nor a single word the mythical misnomer allegedly said retained in the language he would have spoken should he have existed.

Fourth, *Dowd* | David is the returning King of Yisra'el. He is Yahowah's Chosen One, His Firstborn, the Shepherd of God's flock, and the Branch from which the Covenant grows. He is also the *Zarowa'* | Sacrificial Lamb who fulfilled Pesach and Matsah, becoming our *Yatsa'* | Savior. The more we study the *Mizmowr* / Psalms and *Mashal* / Proverbs scribed by this man, the better we will understand what pleases our God.

Fifth, knowing less about Judaism than Christianity, my commentary was originally unbalanced. While Yahowah overtly exposes and condemns my prior faith, God is far more critical of Judaism. Therefore, in an effort to sync my perspective with Yah's, I have endeavored to remove my bias and accept His. Those who read the *Mow'ed* | Appointments volume of *Yada Yahowah* will see the result. My passion is for Yisra'el and Yahuwdah. Therefore, I am committed to correctly conveying Yahowah's antagonism toward the rabbis who have raped His children. The expectation is that many more Jews will walk away from their religion and embrace what it means to be *Yahuwd* | Beloved of Yah.

Sixth, over a decade ago, I came to grips with what I had suspected, that the four vowels which comprise God's name – Y-aH-oW-aH | 𐤉𐤄𐤅𐤄 – are pronounced "Yahowah" not Yahweh or Yahuweh. It should have been obvious since the truth is evident in His *T-oW-R-aH* |

124

Guidance and obvious in *shalowm* and *'elowah*. With these words, He left us with the phonetic tools to properly pronounce every letter in His name. Further, since He told us that His name was based upon the verb "*hayah* – I am," the pronunciation should have been readily apparent.

And seventh, I was comfortable being anonymous and irrelevant, which is why the only name associated with *Yada Yahowah* for a decade or more was Yada – my *nom de plume*. I sought to know Yahowah and then share what I had learned – nothing more. Without exception, I deflected any attention or appreciation directed toward me such that the focus remained on Yahowah.

But that was not what Yahowah intended. God does not like to work alone, and He is consistent when it comes to drawing our attention to those He has chosen to advance His interests. With so many of His people lost in their religion, and with no one else willing, Yahowah not only asked me to work with Him, He spoke vociferously about our collaboration throughout the Towrah, Naby', wa Mizmowr.

𐤋𐤉𐤄𐤅𐤄

There is no endeavor more compassionate or courageous, more enlightened or empowering, more liberating or enriching, than sharing Yahowah's testimony. So, let's review a more succinct recap of the *Shemowth* / Exodus 20 presentation of the Ten Statements prior to completing our study by returning to the Instruction on the Shabat as it was explained by Yahowah in Moseh's presence.

"Then, Almighty God communicated all of these statements composed of words in our presence, in

125

association with us and in proximity to us, providing perspective, explaining…

Tablet One

'I am Yahowah, your God, who, relationally and beneficially to show the correct and narrow path to get the most out of this beneficial relationship, brought you out and delivered you, descending to serve you by doing everything which was required to withdraw those who respond away from the realm of the crucibles of political, religious, economic, and military oppression, out of the house of slavery, away from worship and servitude, government authority and religious officials.

You will not continue to exist with other, different or additional, gods over and above My presence.

You should not continue to associate yourself with or make a practice of attending to, you should not act upon or engage on behalf of a religious image, object of worship, or any representation of a god which is in the heavens above, including the sun, moon, planets, and stars, or which is on the earth below, or which is in the waters beneath the land.

You should not speak about them on your own initiative nor make a practice of bowing down and worshiping them, you should not continue to promote their message on your own accord nor display their words because such uncoerced and ongoing verbal declarations will influence you, and you should not worship them, especially if not compelled, nor should you serve them or encourage anyone to be passionate about them.

Do not continually labor in their cause or make a career of serving as their ministers, nor inspire anyone else to do so.

For, indeed, emphasizing this point, I, Yahowah, your God, am a fiercely protective, steadfastly loyal, and jealous God, a God who is desirous of exclusivity in a devoted relationship.

I consider and reckon the perversity of twisting and distorting and the depravity of perverting and manipulating, deviating from the way, of the fathers upon the children up to the third and the fourth generations of those who are openly adverse toward Me, who are malicious against Me while shunning Me by avoiding a relationship with Me.

And yet, I will genuinely act and actually engage to literally prepare and produce unfailing mercy, unearned favor, and genuine kindness, even actual forgiveness, developing a friendly and loving relationship on behalf of thousands who move toward Me and love Me, forming a close and familial relationship with Me, caring enough to know Me, and also who approach Me by closely observing and carefully considering My instructions, My terms and conditions, the verbal and written stipulations and structure which uphold My Covenant.

You should not continue to deceive, nor should you tolerate or support delusions, you should not habitually deploy or advance clever tricks to enrich yourself by indebting others, and you should avoid beguiling people so that they forget by promoting that which causes them to miss the way by negating the name and reputation of Yahowah, your God, thereby advancing worthless and lifeless deceptions, deploying that which condones devastating dishonesty which nullifies one's existence.

For, indeed, Yahowah will not forgive or leave unpunished, He will not pardon or free from guilt, He will not exempt from judgment or sentencing, an individual who consistently deceives, who actually beguiles and deludes, using religious duplicity to mislead, lifting up or advancing dishonest ruses to forget this association with His name and proper designation, through vain and ineffectual lies which lead to lifelessness.

Tablet Two

Remember to genuinely reflect upon, recognizing that the Shabat, which is the seventh day, is set apart to approach Him.

Six days you should work, laboring for oneself or another, expending the energy to be productive at your job, and choose to act, engaging in all of your service communicating as a heavenly messenger in conjunction with the *Mala'kah* | Spiritual Counselor.

But the seventh, representing the solemn promise which fulfills and satisfies, abundantly enriching those who listen and are observant on this enriching day, the Shabat, the period of reflection on the relationship at the end of the week, is to approach Yahowah, your God.

You should not continuously engage in all of the work of the Heavenly Representative and Spiritual Messenger, yourself, your son, your daughter, your male and female servants and staff, your means of production, as well as those visitors who relationally are in your home or on your property.

For, indeed, in six days, Yahowah acted and engaged and produced everything associated with completing, celebrating and attending to the full extent of the heavens, including the spiritual realm, and the earth, along with the entire material world, even the waters, and all which relationally is in them.

Then, He became completely settled spiritually during the Almighty's seventh day. Therefore, Yahowah blessed and adored, offered a greeting along with an opportunity to meet, favoring everything associated with this day, the Shabat, setting it apart, separating it from that which is common, ordinary, and popular, making it special.

You should choose to carefully consider as worthy, valuable, significant, and highly enriching, perceiving as awesomely impressive, tremendously relevant, and extraordinarily important, even glorious so as to be abundantly enriched and empowered to a very high degree, accordingly, the symbolism of your Father and that which is represented by your Mother for the purpose of continuously lengthening your days upon the earth, which as a benefit of the relationship while revealing the narrow, correct, and straightforward steps to walk along the path to get the most out of life, Yahowah, your God, is actually giving to you.

You should not kill on an ongoing basis, making a practice of taking the life of another whether by accident, revenge, manslaughter, premeditation, assassination, governmental execution, military slaughter, or murder.

You should not continue to participate in idolatrous worship or make a habit of taking another's wife.

You should not make a habit of stealing, routinely taking something from others without their permission.

You should not continuously answer and respond against your neighbor's evil thoughts or the debilitating ways of your countrymen, as a deceptive or misleading, unreliable or useless witness.

You should not make a practice out of desiring, habitually coveting, delighting in or lusting for your troublesome neighbor's home or household.

You should not continuously covet your associate's wife, or his male or female servants, his comings and goings or his domesticated animals, his means of transport, food, and production, or anything which is associated with your maligned countryman's errant opinions or inappropriate behavior.'"

𐤋𐤉𐤄𐤅𐤄

There is an interesting connection between Yahowah's explanation of the Shabat here in *Dabarym* / Words / Deuteronomy 5:15 and Solomon's Sermon on the Mount during the dedication of Yahowah's Temple as presented in *Dabarym ha Yowmym* / Words of the Days / 2nd Chronicles 6:32 which I'd like to share. There appears to be a foreshadowing of something profoundly important to those of us living today. God is announcing and orchestrating a second *Yatsa'* | Exodus – this one from the Babylonian Talmud.

So that you are aware, I am including these insights while editing this *Introduction to God* a decade after I originally wrote it. I have learned so much over the intervening years, I wanted to improve, indeed correct, but mostly augment, what I'd written long ago.

During the ensuing period I have rewritten the initial volume of *An Introduction to God*, edited the first eight volumes of *Yada Yahowah* ten times, completed five volumes of *Twistianity*, compiled five volumes for *Observations*, composed two, eventually three, books entitled *Coming Home*, and have added three volumes entitled *Babel*. I share this with you because my journey from anonymous to prophetically announced began when a citation from Dowd's 5th *Mizmowr* led me to his 20th Psalm. It was something he said that directed our attention to a profoundly important prophecy in *Yasha'yah* 40. In the midst of that translation, one that fundamentally changes our focus away from the mythical misnomer, "Jesus," and toward *Dowd* | David, we found ourselves grappling to find an appropriate definition for *zarowa'*, the same word Yahowah used to explain the purpose of the Shabat.

In search of the truth, I went old school and considered how Yahowah defined *zarowa'* each time He used it. And in so doing, I not only discovered an intriguing range of meanings but also stumbled upon the aforementioned dedication speech which rocked my world – and may change your perspective on what you're reading.

The words we are about to consider were spoken by *Shalomoh* | Reconciliation | Solomon, Dowd's son, upon the completion and commemoration of Yahowah's Family Home. Standing atop Mount *Mowryah* | Moriah with the recently completed Temple in the background, and before all Yisra'el, the man noted for his wisdom, *Shalomoh* | Solomon, delivered the original "Sermon on the Mount."

He was dedicating the building Yahowah had designed to showcase the Ark of the Covenant, these very Tablets of Stone, and the original autograph of the Towrah Moseh had scribed which we have been studying. With Ya'aqob's descendants gathered before him, and speaking of the promises Yahowah had made to his father, *Dowd* | David, while desirous of guiding his people's footsteps, Solomon used an especially descriptive term, *nakry*, which speaks of "a discerning and responsive foreigner from a distant place and time speaking a different language, who, as a result of being observant, would come to understand," to tell the Children of Yisra'el how they should respond to the words this individual would write on their behalf. The timing strongly suggests that they will become especially relevant during a second exodus.

After describing the importance of the Ark of the Covenant which had been placed in the center of God's Home, Solomon reiterated many of the wonderful things which would benefit Yisra'el if the people continued to love Yahowah, sing his father's songs, and observe the *Towrah's* | Guidance. But knowing they would not, realizing that their descendants would require an exodus of their own, Solomon said the following using four especially revealing words…

"**Therefore** (*wa gam* – and in addition), **regarding someone else, an observant and discerning foreigner from a different ethnicity and geographic location who will come to understand** (*ha nakry* – someone from a distant place and unfamiliar culture, speaking a different language, who, having paid attention will comprehend and respond; from *nakar* – someone who, by being attentive and astute will come to be acquainted, recognize, and acknowledge something which deserves our highest regard, respect, and response), **who, to show the way to the benefits of the relationship** (*'asher* – who, to reveal the correct and restrictive path to walk to get the most out of life), **is not of your people** (*lo' min 'am 'atah*), **this Yisra'el** (*Yisra'el huw'*).

He will come (*wa bow'* – he will arrive and enter the scene) **from a distant country in a distant time** (*min 'erets rachowq* – out of a land a great distance from Yisra'el and following a long interval of time) **for the express purpose of being a witness and providing answers regarding** (*lama'an* – for the sake of responding and replying, providing testimony as a witness with the express intent and purpose of revealing) **Your** (*'atah* – 'your' would be *Yahuwdah* | Yah's Beloved while 'Your' would be Yahowah's) **surprisingly important** (*ha gadowl* – tremendously empowering and distinguished, growth-

132

promoting and magnifying, and astonishingly great) **name** (*shem* – personal and proper designation, renown, and reputation), **the influence of Your hand** (*wa yad 'atah* – Your ability to accomplish the mission, especially Your *yad*, the first letter in Your name which as an open hand reaching down and out defines Your role in our lives, denoting Your ability to engage and accomplish the task at hand), **along with the powerful and passionate ruler who is prepared to lead** (*ha chazaq* – the very strong and influential individual with a fighting spirit who is ready and able to protect his people from those who would otherwise seek to harm them, the one who is intensely prepared and resolutely capable of encouraging, repairing, and defending his extended family, the one who embodies the right character, appropriate status, and speaking ability to govern appropriately with a firm and strong hand who clearly knows how to lead in the proper direction (speaking of his father, *Dowd* | David)), **and** (*wa*) **the protective and productive ram who shepherds His flock as well as the sacrificial lamb** (*zarowa' huw'* – the prevailing and effective nature, the strength, resolve, and overall ability of this remarkably important and impactful individual of action who, as a leader and fighter is engaged as a shepherd among his sheep, who is fruitful in his ways, accomplishing the mission, especially when sowing the seeds of truth while denoting and advancing the purpose of the arm of God, of His shepherd and sacrificial lamb (again speaking of his father, *Dowd* | David)) **whom You have extended** (*'atah ha natah* – through whom You have stretched and reached out).

When (*wa*) **he arrives on the scene and chooses to pursue this** (*bow'* – when he (speaking of the *nakry*) comes, bringing and bearing these associations, wanting to clarify the proper direction toward the ultimate goal which is to enter back into the relationship and be included within the family (qal perfect consecutive – literally and genuinely, during this moment in time, and of his own volition)), **then** (*wa*) **he will help interested parties reconcile their relationship by providing those who exercise good judgment with the information and justifications needed to make a correct and reasoned decision** (*palal* – he (the *nakry*) will intervene in the relationship by providing an accurate assessment, enabling thoughtful individuals to come to an agreement, and by foreseeing future events he will provide persuasive arguments which are assured to deliver the expected results) **regarding this familial relationship** (*'el ha beyth ha zeh* – pertaining to and concerning God's home and family (bringing Yisra'el back home, back to Yah's Home in Yaruwshalaim)). (*Dabarym ha Yowmym* / Words of the Days / 2nd Chronicles 6:32)

When you hear this out of the heavens, coming from the atmosphere (*wa 'atah shama' min ha shamaym* – listen to what comes out of the spiritual realm by way of the sky (perhaps prophetic of radio waves and especially satellite-based broadband internet connections from the cloud)) **within the location where you live** (*min makown yashab 'atah* – within the place you are located and dwell), **then** (*wa*) **engage and act accordingly, doing everything** (*'asah ka kol* – under the auspices of freewill, endeavor to expend the considerable effort required to receive all the benefits, doing everything consistent with the example and pattern he has set (qal perfect consecutive)) **which, to show the way** (*'asher* – that, to reveal the proper path to get the most out of life and receive the benefits associated with the relationship), **the observant and responsive foreigner from a different ethnicity and geographic location who understands** (*ha nakry* – this man from a distant place and unfamiliar culture, speaking a distinct language who is uniquely discerning) **has invited you to read** (*qara' 'el 'atah* – has proclaimed and offered to you about God, has recited to you, summoning you to it, calling you out to meet with and be welcomed by God (qal imperfect – literally with unfolding consequences)), **for the express purpose**

of being a witness, who provides answers such that (*lama'an* – for the sake of responding, providing testimony with the express intent and purpose of revelation such that) **all peoples of the earth** (*kol 'am ha 'erets* – everyone, every family and nation of the material realm) **will have a genuine and ongoing opportunity to become familiar with, to know, acknowledge, accept, and understand** (*yada'* – will be shown by Yada' so that they might appreciate and comprehend (qal imperfect – genuinely and actually on an ongoing basis)) **Your name** (*'eth shem 'atah* – that which is associated with Your proper designation and actual reputation), **coming to respect and revere You** (*wa la yare' 'eth 'atah* – once revitalized, will approach Your awesome nature) **simultaneously along with** (*ka* – concurrently with) **Your people** (*'am 'atah*), **Yisra'el** (*Yisra'el* – Individuals who Struggle and Wrestle or Engage and Endure with God).

And also so that (*wa la*) **they may know** (*yada'* – they might acknowledge, accept, and understand) **that, truthfully** (*ky* – assuredly), **Your family and this House** (*'al ha beyth ha zeh* – that Your Home), **which to reveal the correct path to walk to give life meaning that** (*'asher* – to show the way to benefit from the relationship) **I have built for the family** (*banah* – I [Shalomoh] have constructed for the generations, for the son and the son's son), **who are designated and called** (*qara'* – is summoned and received, proclaimed and appointed, and especially called out and welcomed) **by Your name** (*shem 'atah* – by Your proper designation, Your reputation and renown (*Yahuwdah* – Yahowah's Beloved))." (*Dabarym ha Yowmym* / Words of the Days / 2nd Chronicles 6:33)

With Solomon's speech still reverberating in my mind, it became immediately obvious that his declaration drew inspiration from Moseh's presentation of the Shabat during the *Yatsa'* | Exodus for a reason. These four words appear, one after the other, in both statements: *chazaq*, *yad*, *zarowa'*, and *natah*. I don't think that it was by accident.

"**So** (*wa*), **you should remember** (*zakar* – you should call to mind, recollect, mention, and actually proclaim at this moment in time (qal perfect)) **that, indeed** (*ky*), **you were** (*hayah* – you existed as (qal perfect)) **a slave** (*'ebed* – a servant owned by another) **in the land** (*ba 'erets* – in the realm and country) **of the Crucibles of Political and Religious Oppression** (*Mitsraym* – the cauldrons of military, economic, conspiratorial, societal, and governmental persecution and subjugation; plural of *matsowr* – to be considered inferior and besieged during a time of testing and tribulation, from *tsuwr* – to be bound and confined by an adversary, assaulted, shut up, and enclosed as if in a concentration camp by those showing great hostility) **and** (*wa* – then) **Yahowah** (*Yahowah* – the proper pronunciation of YaHoWaH, our *'elowah* – God as directed in His *ToWRaH* – teaching regarding His *HaYaH* – existence and our *ShaLoWM* – restoration), **your God** (*'elohy 'atah*), **brought you out, withdrawing you** (*yatsa' 'atah* – descended and extended Himself, came forth to lead and deliver you, taking you (hifil imperfect)) **from there** (*min sham | shem* – out of and away from that place called by this name and having that reputation) **with** (*ba* – by and in) **a mighty and firm, powerful and protective** (*chazaq* – very strong and influential, extraordinarily capable and intensely prepared, resolutely passionate and encouraging, assertive and aggressive, feisty and steadfast) **hand** (*yad* – ability to accomplish the mission, a *yad* – the first letter in Yah's name which as an open hand reaching down and out, defining Yah's role in our lives, denoting His ability to engage and accomplish the task at hand), **and with** (*wa ba*) **the Productive Ram, the Strong Arm Shepherding the Flock** (*zarowa'* – the prevailing and effective nature, the strength, resolve, and overall ability of this remarkably important and impactful individual of action who, as a leader and fighter is engaged as a shepherd among his sheep, who is fruitful in his ways, accomplishing the mission, especially when sowing the seeds of truth while denoting and advancing the purpose of the arm of God, of His shepherd and sacrificial lamb) **extended** (*natah* – reaching out).

For this reason (*'al ken* – upon these grounds above all others, it is right, therefore, that), **Yahowah** (*YaHoWaH* – an accurate presentation of the name of *'elowah* – God as guided by His *towrah* – instructions regarding His *hayah* – existence)**, your God** (*'elohy 'atah*)**, instructed you** (*tsawah 'atah* – directed you (piel perfect)) **to approach by observing** (*la shamar* – to move toward and draw near, by closely examining and carefully considering (qal infinitive construct – a literal descriptive verb and genuine actionable noun)) **that which is associated with the day** (*'eth yowm*) **of the Shabat** (*ha shabat* – the seventh day, the period of reflection on the relationship at the end of the week, reminiscent of the promise of settling debts so we can settle down by observing the oath of association; from *shaba'* – fulfilling and satisfying the promise of seven to abundantly empower and enrich) **such that it is set apart and special** (*'eth qodesh* – so that it is uncommon, cleansing, and perfecting)." (*Dabarym* 5:15)

As I write this to you in the summer of 2023, the ultimate celebration of the Shabat commences on *Kipurym* | Reconciliations in the *Yowbel* | Year of the Lamb of God in 6000 Yah (sunset in Yaruwshalaim on October 2nd, 2033) is just ten years away – some of which will transpire during the Time of Ya'aqob's Troubles. For Yahowah to fulfill His promise to reconcile His relationship with His people there must be another *Yatsa'* | Exodus, this one away from crucibles of political, religious, and geographic Babylon: the United States of America, the Roman Catholic Church, and the lands now infected by Islam – as well as from the Haredim and their Babylonian Talmud.

There is precious little time left to bring Yisra'el and Yahuwdah back home, back to the Promised Land.

Sadly, there wasn't a single willing Yahuwd through whom Yahowah could convey this message, which means that there would be no prophet or shepherd for His people at this time, as there was with Moseh and Dowd. But there would, nonetheless, be a witness, a *nakry*, who would write what those seeking to be with Yahowah would need to *qara'* | read and *yada'* | know. He would translate Yahowah's Testimony, and that of Moseh and Dowd, the words of the Hebrew Towrah and Prophets, into English – the language spoken by more people today, including "Jews," than any other.

There does not appear to be another candidate for this role in our presence or on the horizon. And since there isn't time for one to emerge and compile the requisite translations and insights, you may want to ponder why Yahowah made this prophetic announcement regarding the *nakry* and then consider why Solomon included part of the Dabarym presentation on the Shabat and Exodus in his prophetic declaration. If they are addressing this time and these translations, then you are in the right place, and if not, reading more of what Yahowah had to say so that you can respond appropriately is always a good idea.

𐤋𐤉𐤄𐤅𐤄

RESOURCES

YadaYah.com

BlogTalkRadio.com/Yada

Facebook: *Facebook.com/YadaYahowah*

X: *X.com/YadaYahowah*

Instagram: *Instagram.com/YadaYahowah*

YouTube: *YouTube.com/@YadaYahowah*

Rumble: *Rumble.com/YadaYahowah*

Amazon Music: *Yada Yah Radio*

Apple Podcasts: *Yada Yah Radio*

Printed Books: *Amazon.com (Craig Winn)*

Contact: *email@YadaYah.com*

Cover photo from *www.shutterstock.com*

Ver. 20241121

Printed in Great Britain
by Amazon